PAINS ON TRAINS

FOR EMBATTLED COMMUTERS EVERYWHERE...

PAINS ON TRAINS

A COMMUTER'S GUIDE TO THE 50 MOST IRRITATING TRAVEL COMPANIONS

ANDREW HOLMES AND MATTHEW REEVES

CAPSTONE

First published 2003 by
Capstone Publishing Limited (A Wiley Company)
The Atrium, Southern Gate, Chichester,
West Sussex PO19 8SQ, United Kingdom
e-mail: info@wiley-capstone.co.uk
www.capstoneideas.com

Reprinted November 2003, December 2003

CIP catalogue records for this book are available from the British Library and the US Library of Congress

ISBN 1-84112-564-4

Designed and typeset by Baseline, Oxford, UK
Printed and bound by T.J. International
This book is printed on acid-free paper

Substantial discounts on bulk quantities of Capstone books are available to corporations, professional
associations and other organisations.

For details telephone John Wiley and Sons on +44 (0)1243-770441 or (fax) +44 (0)1243-770571
or (e-mail) info@wiley-capstone.co.uk

Contents

Preface	6	THE MAMMOTH	112
Acknowledgements	8	THE MOBILE PHONER	116
TRIAL BY COMMUTING	10	THE NEW WORKER	120
THE BEGGAR	16	THE NIGHT CLUBBERS	124
THE BELLIGERENT	20	THE NOSE PICKER	128
THE BORN IN A STABLE	24	THE NUTTER	132
THE BROADSHEET	28	THE OVER YOUR SHOULDER	136
THE CITY BOY	32	THE PERVERT	140
THE CLIQUE	36	THE PHANTOM FARTER	144
THE CREATIVE	40	THE RESERVIST	148
THE DEADBEAT	44	THE RITUALIST	152
THE DEATH BREATH	48	THE SARDINE PACKER	156
THE DOUBLE SEATER	52	THE SLEEPER	160
THE DRUNK	56	THE SOCIAL CLIMBER	164
THE ENGAGER	60	THE SPINSTER	168
THE ENQUIRER	64	THE STARER	172
THE FAMILY	68	THE STINKER	176
THE FAST FOODER	72	THE STRETCHER	180
THE FLAMBOYANT GROIN	76	THE TERRITORIALIST	184
THE GADGET	80	THE TEXTER	188
THE GAGGLE	84	THE TOFF	192
THE GROUP	88	THE TRAIN TIMER	196
THE HERO	92	THE TRAVELLER	200
THE HIGH-FLIER	96	THE VOMITER	204
THE LATE STARTER	100	THE WHEELED CASER	108
THE LOVERS	104	THE YOUTH	212
THE MAKE UP ARTIST	108	Afterword	216

Preface

It was one of those rare days. Work had been enjoyable and I was in a good mood. That morning I had spent time busying myself with clients and had even managed to steal myself some time to discuss my latest ideas with my publisher. I got to the station in plenty of time, expecting to unwind on the commute home. Pointless, I know, but I can dream. Not surprisingly the train was late, untidy and filled with the usual mixture of people with whom I would not choose to spend any time, let alone a fifty-minute train journey. I settled in my seat, thumbed to my place in my book and began reading.

Not long into the journey, it started. The guy opposite on his mobile, addressing the entire carriage. "I can't believe it! The Evening Standard have just published my article! It's fantastic, I'm so pleased!" Okay, I thought, I'll cut the guy some slack, as having a piece in the evening newspaper might be the apogee of his writing career. Perhaps he was on the phone to his wicked, self-centred mother whom he wanted to impress, or maybe his boyfriend. I didn't know. To be frank, I didn't care. But it didn't stop. No sooner was one call finished than the next began, repeating the same words over and over again (had he been rehearsing in the toilet all day?). Now, either the chap concerned had plenty of friends, or he was calling people randomly to demonstrate to the rest of us how literary he was. And I do bow to his achievement, you understand. It's not every day you have something published in the Standard. Yet I would wager on the second option. His voice was so loud. Was that blood trickling from the ears of his neighbour? Everyone in the carriage had to endure his attempts to impress – surely there was no other reason for so much noise over such a trivial event.

I took time to look at him. Couldn't help it really, given the spectacle he was making of himself. He was what I call a Creative (you'll see more of him later), all in black: black polo neck, black jacket, a pair of black shades in his top pocket on this dark winter evening (but maybe he had an eye complaint). And, like this genre of people, his jacket showed off his dandruff; a light smattering, but enough to show that he had a problem. I was not alone in my contempt. Another traveller leant towards me and remarked "What a tosser!" I bonded with a suitable expletive. Although our exchange had been sufficiently vocal for the Creative to overhear, it made not a jot of difference, as he continued bellowing his wonderful news for the entire train journey.

But every cloud has a silver lining. It struck me that commuting life is made more miserable by some of the characters who travel on the trains. On studying my fellow commuters more closely, I noticed there were many different types of annoying people, some more common than others, some certainly more irritating and some even amusing. Virtually everyone tolerates them and only rarely does anyone make a stand. Then revenge came to me, like a bolt from the blue. Pains on Trains, that's it! – fighting back on behalf of the embattled commuter who can derive some entertainment value at the expense of those who make a bad journey still worse. I would, of course, like to thank the clod who made this particular journey especially bad. Without his help I would still be gritting teeth and rolling my eyes. If only I could be bothered to find out his name...

AH

Acknowledgements

Writing this book has been a real departure from the usual material I turn my hand to. All my other books to date have been on business subjects, scholarly and practical. Creating them involves input from a small number of key thinkers. This book has been very different. When I mentioned the concept to my friends, family, colleagues and anyone who would listen, their eyes lit up as they responded "Have you got the person who...they really annoy me!" and "Here's a story for this Pain". It was obvious I had hit a raw nerve and it seemed that everyone wanted to have their say. So I would like to thank the many people who added their input, including James McColl, George Stevenson, Linda Latham, Isambard Kingdom Brunel, Richard Hartley, Chris Frost, Michael Storrier, Linda Bowman, Dr. Beeching, Ken Wareham, Nick Birks, Phil Highe, Bart Smith, Martin Lloyd, Andy Wicks, Zoe George, successive governments who have underinvested in our railways, Andy Baggott, Peter Mussett, Donna Peters, William Huskisson (the first person to suffer from train travel), Godert van der Poel, Nigel Albon, Stephanie Hyner, Michael Campbell, Simon Viney and of course all the anonymous commuters who have unwittingly provided the role models of the Pains contained within this book.

I would like to pick out a few people for particular attention. First to Richard Burton at Capstone who believed the idea was a winner. Second to Philip Read who put me in contact with Matt Reeves, who has done such a fantastic job of capturing my perspectives on commuting life in such striking images. Thirdly to Nick Birks who was kind enough to read through my early manuscript and provide some very constructive comments. And finally to Sally, my wife, who although initially sceptical, recognised I had this type of book in me and added her usual critical and valuable input.

Trial by commuting

"*Pains breach the accepted understanding that train travel should be a silent, contemplative pursuit; the bread slices that cushion the work sandwich.*"
– Nick Birks

Recent research into happiness has shown that we are at our least happy during the morning commute to work and not much happier coming home. This degree of unhappiness is, of course, closely followed by work itself so there may be some degree of correlation. According to the same research we at our happiest when having sex. So the only way we can enjoy our commute is to have sex at the same time. And, as we shall see, some people do.

THE MORNING HUSTLE

The six o'clock alarm shocks you awake. It's a bleak Monday morning, and you have another great day at work ahead of you. Many of us will sigh at the prospect of scraping ourselves out of bed at such an ungodly hour and I do wonder just who would work, given the choice. Not many, I imagine. There are of course a happy few who see it as the pinnacle of self-actualisation, but most of us pursue our 'careers' through economic necessity, nothing more and nothing less. But this book isn't about the joys, or otherwise of work, so let's move on. You've grabbed some breakfast, fed the children, rushed out of the door, and driven to the station (or been ferried there by a dutiful partner). It's time to get on the train. You make your way along the station platform to precisely the same place you did the day before, the day before that, and the day before that. In fact for the whole of your commuting life. It is said we are creatures of habit. If nothing else commuting reinforces this widely held view.

Depending on the time of your train, you may stand at different places along the platform. If it's the early train, perhaps you will stand at one end. If the later train, the other. Everyone has their spot. The next time you make your way to your chosen position, cast a glance across the people up and down the platform. They are the same ones you see every day. Each of them depressed, cold, dejected and generally pissed off to be standing, yet again, on the same bloody platform at the same bloody station. Groundhog Day has nothing on this. I don't know whether it's a blessing or a pity that no one speaks. They have been taking the same journey for years and still they do not acknowledge anyone around them, let alone talk to them. It's odd, given that we spend more time with these people than we do with our family and friends. They view each other with disdain and suspicion and in any case are probably too caught up in their own petty worlds of work; it's trivial and meaningless to be concerned about anyone else. My sister-in-law loves to play games with the platform lemmings (as she calls them). From time to time she will move from her usual platform position to another. This creates fear, uncertainty and doubt in minds of those left. "Does she know something we don't?" "Is this a shorter train than normal?" "Oh, bugger, does this mean I won't be getting a seat?" Everyone shifts uncomfortably from side to side, not knowing what to do. They think to themselves "If only someone else would make a move, then maybe I could." They display true herd instincts. Usually of course there is nothing abnormal about the train, and if they had moved position, they would have lost their seat. The same is true when it is a rainy day. Everyone cowers under the safe haven of the covered platform and waits like runners on the starting block for the train to appear. No one dares to move, but as soon as one brave soul decides to go for it, everyone follows like sheep being rounded up by the sheepdog.

All of us stand impassively and apprehensively, hoping there will be enough seats. Standing for fifty minutes is not the best way to start your day, but it is a real prospect for most. As the train pulls in, knuckles whiten as heartbeats and blood pressure rise. Loins are girded for the scramble to come. Men and women jostle for an optimum position as near to the door as possible, whilst those at the back attempt to squirrel their way through to the front. If you have negotiated this nerve-racking process to secure a seat, you can draw breath ready to settle into your relaxing journey into work. Indeed it's time to get this book out and begin your now favourite pastime of Pain Spotting.

Having sat, or for those unlucky in the seat lottery, stood or squatted your way to your destination you now have to endure the long march to your final resting place – work. But even leaving the train and walking down the platform is a dangerous and at times infuriating affair. You have to contend with the Darters who move at a hundred miles an hour dashing between people. They are either genuinely excited by another day at the office or have a desperate need to empty their bowels. The Darters will bump you aside, oblivious to your presence. Then there are the congenital Smokers who light up as soon as their lungs are exposed to fresh air. You are caught in the blue cloud created when they pause to light up. As you try to move past, you get a final waft only to find there is another one in front. And we shouldn't forget the Wheeled Caser (more of them later) trundling up the platform like an elderly lady with a shopping trolley. The wake they leave appears to be a prized island of tranquillity unclaimed by others until you get your feet caught by the case as it castors on its precarious way. By the size of some of these, they may well be used for some mysterious trade in dead bodies. But taking the kitchen sink to work makes them look important. And finally, although I could go on, there is the Zig Zagger who can't make up their mind which way they are going. Is it left, right, forwards or backwards? No one knows. Perhaps they are controlled remotely by an evil station attendant just to finish you off before the daily grind. No matter how you might try to anticipate them, they will thwart you at the last minute, blocking your escape route. Then once outside of the station, you contend with the beggars, buskers, canvassers and anyone else who thinks you are going to part with your well-earned cash. All of this infinite monotony is soul destroying and pointless. Clearly, for many of us, making it into the office is a Herculean task. But don't forget, you have to get home again.

THE EVENING DÉNOUEMENT

At the end of the day, when you have dealt with all the nightmares on your desk, had your ritual humiliation from the boss, motivated your staff and spent the vast majority of the time surfing the Internet, abusing the phone system, sending emails to your mates, and oh yes, doing some work, you have the joy of trying to get home. Just like the morning, you stand along with everyone else waiting like lemmings, heads upwards staring blankly at the indicator boards, hoping to find out when (or if) your train will depart. Then when it is time, you rush towards the ticket gates desperately hoping to get your seat. Pushing, shoving, kicking and sometimes punching your way first onto the platform and then onto the train.

Anything to get a double seat. Habit again takes over. Do you sit in the middle of the train so that you can be near the exit when you pull into your station, or do you walk to the end where you can get some peace and quiet and, most importantly, a double seat? But, don't worry, whatever you do you will have ample opportunity to continue Pain Spotting. Only when you reach the sanctuary of your home can you finally relax and recover ready for the next day.

USING THIS BOOK

This book, if you hadn't already figured it out, is all about those people who aggravate you on your daily commute. It designed in a way that allows you to spot your most hated commuter whilst at the same time expressing your own inner feelings in an accessible and light-hearted way. I am writing what you are thinking. Thus, in the same way that bird spotters identify the lesser spotted warbler, this book helps you to spot the Broadsheet, Engager and Family. But it goes beyond that, as it identifies how you can avoid them and seek your revenge if you are brave enough; not the sort of thing you find in the average bird spotting tome, unless you are armed with a shotgun. Each entry in Pain Spotting includes:

* The general characteristics of the Pain (including anecdotes and stories from fellow travellers)
* Their annoyance rating, which rates the Pain from 1 (limited annoyance) to 10 (extreme annoyance)
* Their rarity, which rates the Pain form 1 (exceptionally rare) to 10 (very common)
* Any seasonal variations, which will identify any seasonal changes to the Pain
* A range of avoidance/revenge strategies (with suitable escalation).

Long gone are the days when Jimmy Saville (for those of us old enough to remember him) would say with a cheerful voice "let the train take the strain". These days, it's "Let the train take the Pain". Read on and become one of the growing army of Pain Spotters. Maybe we'll meet at a Pain Spotting convention sometime soon.

Matt and I hope you enjoy this book. We are planning other volumes, including Pains on the Payroll and Pains in Public. The next two volumes will allow you to track how people can change from one Pain to another and build The Complete Guide to Pain Spotting, something you will cherish for decades to come. So if you would like to vote for and promote your favourite Pain at work or in public, then why not email Matt and I with your contributions and stories at pains_on@hotmail.com.

At the end of each entry I have also given you, the reader, an opportunity to record that you have spotted the Pain and add your own annoyance rating. Like any 'spotting' pastime, it has to be interactive, fun and have a sense of purpose to it. You might choose to swap entries with your friends and families and, God forbid, your fellow commuters. All you will need then is a brown anorak to feel right at home. You might also choose to wrap the book in brown paper to disguise your antics.

The Beggar...

GENERAL CHARACTERISTICS

Sure, we can all fall on hard times, and care in the community programmes mean more vulnerable people have to cope for themselves. But no one likes beggars. However watching peoples' behaviour when a Beggar works a carriage is always an absorbing experience. Most will do their utmost to avoid eye contact with them in the hope that they will be ignored. Fat chance. A few will actively engage the Beggar in direct conversation, quizzing them on their predicament and offering them some moral support and the odd piece of fruit. Unfortunately for the majority who attempt to evade the Beggar, they usually fail because the Beggar is an expert at grabbing peoples' attention. The Beggar is always filthy, you know the sort of thing, black hands, dirty face, probably skid marked pants and of course smelly. They often carry cans of Special Brew or cider and swig the drink as they stagger up and down the carriage asking for some spare change. They say this is for a cup of tea but by the look of them it is probably for their next fix of crack cocaine. It's no wonder everyone wants to avoid them. They usually make statements such as "I was in the last Gulf War" or "The Police have kicked me off the streets again. I can't understand it, why aren't they sorting out the drug dealers?" When it comes to securing money from the poor passengers, they adopt one of two strategies. First they will attempt to *entertain* you with a cacophony of crass music or singing. I have seen beggars using traffic cones as instruments, dressing up as animals and using old tins to amuse the commuters.

On conclusion of their act, they walk around pushing their disgusting flesh into the faces of the cowering passengers in the hope of being paid for their efforts. Of course very few people oblige. Most say "I'm sorry, I haven't got any change," as they try to avoid their cash jingling in their pockets. Others look down at their crotch hoping to see something more interesting. A few of course will feel suitably embarrassed and pass the Beggar a few pence. And when this is not enough it is usually followed by some expletive like "Is that all, you F***ing tightwad!" Because the Beggar is, by and large, pretty unsuccessful they move along quite quickly and eventually into the adjoining carriage. This is usually followed by a collective sigh of relief. There are other variants of the Beggar which can be more sinister including the women with a baby, the unemployed foreigner, or the particularly menacing thug. I was told of one foreigner who was working the first class carriage of a busy train. When he came to a friend of mine he placed a card which said "I am an Croatian refugee and I need some money for some food" onto his laptop (he could, of course, speak no English). When my friend failed to oblige, he picked up the card and got of the train. Only when the doors had shut did my friend realise that the Beggar had taken his mobile phone as well. The Tube is a particularly good place to spot the Beggar mainly because it is metropolitan. The Tramp is a variant of the Beggar who, judging by the following story, should be avoided at all costs. A tramp got onto the Tube with an ice cream and sat between two well-dressed commuters, one male and the other female, and began to lick away at his cone. Both the man and the women eased themselves away from the tramp as much as they could as the smell was unbearable. Unfortunately, the tramp sneezed and streams of phlegm went everywhere, on the lady, the man and on the tramp and his ice cream. As if this wasn't bad enough the tramp carried on eating his ice cream even though it was now topped off with some rather large globules of snot. At least he didn't ask for any money.

ANNOYANCE RATING

8 – looking at the reaction from the commuters who end up being entertained by the Beggar you can see that most are upset by their presence. I guess most of this stems from the abhorrence that someone could exist in such an appalling state and that this was being pushed into their faces. Let's face it, most of us like to lead our lives in bubbles where we pretend that everything is good in the world. We all like to act as if beggars don't exist. So when they do appear we feel somewhat guilty. This is not lost on the Beggar who will often carry a moth-eaten blanket or have a scraggy-looking dog by his side secured with a piece of rope. All help to increase the sympathy vote but do little to improve their cashflow.

RARITY

2 – The Beggar is pretty rare on the trains. You tend to find more of them on the Tube in London and in those provincial cities that have underground systems. You will also find them on the Metro in France, although you have to be fluent in French to understand them.

SEASONAL VARIATIONS

Winter will bring out more Beggars than the summer because of the cold weather. The **bitter winds** and the **driving rain** will force them to find warmth and what better place than the train or underground system.

AVOIDANCE / REVENGE STRATEGIES

1. Sew up your pockets.

2. Offer them the telephone number of the Big Issue so that they can pull themselves out of the gutter.

3. Give them a bar of soap and tell them to get a wash.

4. Pretend to be a foreign visitor and take their photograph as a memento of your visit.

5. Smear your self with mud and wear shabby clothes so that you won't be accosted

☐ Tick here when you have spotted the Beggar

RATE THE
BEGGAR'S
ANNOYANCE

The Belligerent

GENERAL CHARACTERISTICS

There are a lot of angry people in this world. The pressures of work, poor or failing marriages and mundane existences have the capacity to turn us all into loose cannons. You might think this was bad enough, but transport has the ability to tip us over the edge and none so more than trains. The Belligerent is a very angry person who you want to avoid if you can. However, as long as the belligerence is not directed towards you, they can offer some very hilarious diversions. As is often the case, we do not find many Belligerents on the way into work, but plenty on the way home. My financial advisor was travelling home one evening, around seven o'clock. The ticket inspector was making his rounds when he came to a couple of women (in their mid twenties). "I'm sorry, these tickets are not valid," he said. "What do you mean, they are not valid? They let us through the barrier!" they replied "I'm sorry, they are not valid for this line, they are for the Fenchurch line. You'll have to pay ten pounds each." "But it let me through the barrier, it is valid!" said one of the women. This toing and froing went on for a few more minutes. Then the ticket inspector said "You'll have to pay up." "I can't," came the reply. "Then you'll have to give me your name and address." "I'll give you a false one." "Then in that case you'll have to provide some proof of identity." "I'm not going to!" Then someone interjected further down the carriage "Just pay the money, you f***ing slut". Then an old woman piped up: "I think it is appalling how people avoid paying for their tickets." The incensed women retaliated "Yeah, and you're the type who probably sits in the toilet and hides

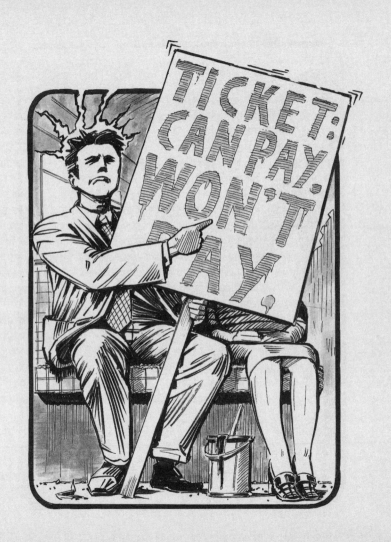

rather than pay for your ticket, you old bag*!*" A guy further down the carriage then shouted "Shut up, you slut*!*" The ticket inspector diverted his attention to the man shouting and asked him to calm down. He replied "Look, I've got my ticket. Let's look at it. Does it say that I can't shout on the train – no*!* Is there a by-law that says it is forbidden to shout on the train – no*!*" It was clearly not the ticket inspector's day. Having resolved the issue he moved back the way he came. Then a group of people who had said nothing throughout the entire episode piped up. "You're going the wrong way. You haven't checked the tickets at this end of the train," "What's a matter, aren't our tickets good enough for you?*!*" and "I'll know where to sit next time, then, won't I*!*" It is rare to experience such a collective vent, but, boy, what entertainment. I often see heated exchanges between single commuters complaining about tickets and train times. Their anger knows no bounds as they shout, swear and verbally abuse the ticket inspector until he moves on. People often shout and complain to the stewards who are not even employed by the train company. One man who shares my commute is particularly prone to have a go. He will complain and shout about everything and looks as though he will be dropping dead of a heart attack anytime soon. I see him pacing up and down, shouting at the platform attendants, steam coming out from his ears, his red face like a beetroot as he complains yet again. Chill out, there is no point in fighting the system. Do what the rest of us do, sit there in a state of depressed acceptance.

ANNOYANCE RATING

1 – I find the Belligerent enjoyable and I admire them because they are willing to have a go when no one else will. Most of us have been so crushed by the system that we just accept the crap that is dealt out to us. But the Belligerent will not give up without a fight. Good on them.

RARITY

5 – As we all get more in touch with our emotional and feminine side, we will become better at kicking out and turning on our belligerence when we need to. This will help us deal with the deterioration in service that we have come to accept. I would love the Belligerent to become the most popular Pain because it is time the poor commuter fought back. But we do have to guard against Train Rage.

SEASONAL VARIATIONS

Although **poor service all year** round is enough to get the Belligerent going, the **winter months** are when you will spot more of them. Service levels drop considerably during wet and cold weather as does our ability to deal with it. It's all to do with a lack of sun, you know. So just as people can suffer from seasonal adjustment disorder, so can train travellers, although this is commonly known in medical circles as seasonal train disorder and I believe is a notifiable disease.

AVOIDANCE / REVENGE STRATEGIES

1. Never clean your ears so that they are so stuffed with wax you can't hear anything.

2. Take Prozac.

3. Film the Belligerent in action and send it into "Train Journeys from hell".

4. Spray mace at them.

5. Use riot foam to stop the situation from escalating.

☐ Tick here when you have spotted the Belligerent

RATE THE **BELLIGERENT'S** ANNOYANCE

The Born in a Stable

GENERAL CHARACTERISTICS

My mother always used to tell me to shut the door after myself when I came into the room and when I failed to do so asked if I was born in a stable. After many years of having this message drummed into me I feel that I now act responsibly when faced with an open door (my wife would and does disagree with this statement). But judging by the prevalence of the Born in a Stable, I don't think many others have. The good news is that advances in rolling stock means that they are a dying breed. Indeed, one day they may well become extinct. I look forward to seeing David Attenborough's *Life of Commuters* in which he traces the life and death of commuting mammals. The Born in a Stable is a careless and sloppy thinker, more worried about whether they will be getting a seat, or depositing their waste products, than the trivia of shutting doors behind them. Their nature and impact will vary according to the type of train they travel on. Slam door trains are the worst. The carriages on these trains have internal doors that require the commuter to pull them shut. Many don't bother, or find it too hard to do so. So they leave them open. The slam door trains are also notoriously draughty at the best of times, but during the winter months they are positively icy. Leaving the door open is a cardinal sin and reactions are typical. Having one person leave the door open is bad enough but a whole stream is especially aggravating. You only need to look at the poor sod's face who is constantly having to lean over and shut the door, each time harder than the last.

This is usually accompanied by heavy sighs and barely audible muttering. Their entire journey is punctuated by them shutting the door.

Those who use slam door trains also have problems shutting the exterior doors. They climb on with all their paraphernalia and leave the door wide open or on the latch. Yet again we have to pull the door shut. Modern trains also present opportunities for the Born in a Stable, especially the toilets. The loos on these trains tend to be automatic, why I don't know. Just a pointless innovation which is subject to defects and breakdowns. And for some strange reason there is often a seat directly outside, which means you are subject to wafts of urine and faeces each time the door is left open. It is an endless source of amusement to watch people who are clearly desperate to relieve themselves struggle to shut a malfunctioning door. Their eyes bulge as panic sets in when they realise that if the door doesn't stop soon they will need to visit an underwear store to replace their soiled undergarments. I even remember one woman having the door open on her whilst on the job. There she was knickers on the floor, skirt hoisted up above her waist, hands on her chin focusing on the job in hand. She screamed in horror. The moral of this story is not to use automatic toilets.

There is another variant of the Born in a Stable and this is the Window Opener. Not satisfied with leaving every door open, the Window Opener will typically be someone who has run for the train, feels incredibly hot and bothered and assumes quite wrongly that the rest of the carriage could benefit from having a number of windows open. What they forget is that everyone else has disrobed and is perfectly content with the windows shut. One commuter told me of one woman who got on a train, sat in the middle seat of three and opened the window. The lady on the inside seat, without looking up from her book, stretched up her arm and banged it shut. The first woman sat chastened for the rest of the journey without saying a word.

ANNOYANCE RATING

7 – the annoyance rating will vary according to where you are sitting and the time of year. If you are sitting near a door and it is winter or outside one of the automatic toilets then it can be very unpleasant. In the summer the worst place to be is by the toilets. The stench is unbelievable. I do wonder what people have eaten.

RARITY

6 – The Born in a Stable will undoubtedly die out as the technical sophistication of the trains ensures doors are automatically shut once you pass through them. For the time being however, they are quite common and especially so on the old slam door trains. As we know, these trains were meant to be replaced, but due to the lack of power to the tracks it is likely that we will have to suffer them for quite some time to come. How long it takes for the Born in a Stable to become extinct will therefore depend almost entirely on the train line you happen to commute on.

SEASONAL VARIATIONS

I have not witnessed much in the way of seasonal variation, as this is a factor of **upbringing** and **attitude** rather than season. With so many working parents failing to bring up their darling children with proper manners, I can't see much of a shift in door-shutting behaviour. Thankfully, the greater numbers of automatic doors will shield us from them, assuming they work of course.

AVOIDANCE / REVENGE STRATEGIES

1. Sit away from all doors.

2. Produce some "Please shut the door" signs and place them around the carriage.

3. Sit next to the Mammoth so you are shielded from the blasts of cold air as the door is left open.

4. Play farmyard noises on your portable stereo to make them feel more at home.

5. Once in your favourite spot, secure the doors with a padlock and chain so that no one else can get in.

☐ Tick here when you have spotted the Born in a Stable

RATE THE **BORN IN A STABLE'S** ANNOYANCE

The Broadsheet

It's the morning commute, you have survived the misery of rain, fog, snow (and occasionally heat) to get onto the train. You have even managed to find a seat, which is a major achievement. Then you meet them; The Broadsheet. These people are the bane of many a commuter's life and arguably the biggest Pain that appears in the morning rush. There are in fact few others as most people are too tired, depressed or brain dead to raise much more than a grunt before lunchtime. There is something particularly annoying about the Broadsheet. After all, you expect the great unwashed to reveal their inner qualities on the commute home, but surely not in the morning? The only civil, self-contemplative time you have left before work. The very nature of the quality paper pretty much guarantees you will be annoyed – after all have you ever tried to read a broadsheet paper in a confined space? To be frank it is almost impossible unless you fold it into four – but that's comical in its own right; watching someone struggle reading a couple of columns at a time and then desperately unfolding and refolding their paper like an origami artist is a great way to spend forty minutes. Couple your annoyance with the general arrogance and superiority of the Broadsheet and you have all the ingredients for a miserable journey into work. I don't know why they have the right to feel so superior. Maybe it's because the average reading ability of those around them is that of a seven year old, or maybe it's because they want to elevate themselves above the 'little people' who don't aspire to reading something so intellectual so early in the morning. The

Broadsheet will deliberately seek to occupy as much of your space as they can. They will extend their arms into your face, their paper will knock into you and its edge will flop over you as you read or work. You will be forced to shift to the edge of the seat or lean out of their way, guaranteeing that you will compress your spine or pull a muscle. But the truly annoying thing about the Broadsheet comes when they sit at a table. In this position, they can annoy two people simultaneously: the person next to them and the one opposite. They will sit there with a smug smile on their face oblivious to the disruption they cause. What is more fascinating is the paper itself, as this suggests something about the person reading it.

The Guardian – trendy leftist, who supports social re-engineering but still likes his six figure income. The Guardian reader likes to pretend they are concerned about the social welfare of those around them, but in the main they are there for the pose and out for themselves. They normally dress like tramps, have unkempt hair and like to pose as pseudo-intellectuals

The Financial Times - clearly suggests that the reader is in finance, the city, posing or is independently wealthy (although why would they want to be on a packed train, nobody knows). These people like to believe they are a cut above the rest and usually look the part. Superior and retentive, a fine combination.

The Telegraph – someone who holds right wing views, but has the reading age of more than a seven year old (otherwise they would be reading The Sun). And like the Tory party, they have lost their way.

The Times – a true member of the middle class who probably doesn't aspire to much, but is reliable, dependable and a fine upstanding member of society

The Independent – a dull person without any views at all.

The **Broadsheet** can get a lot worse when coupled with other **Pains**, such as the **Territorialist** or the **Mammoth**. In such instances, you end up with less space than is legally permissible for a guinea pig.

ANNOYANCE RATING

8 – The Broadsheet never ceases to annoy, but the worst thing is when they hunt in packs.

RARITY

9 – The Broadsheet is very common and is almost exclusively a morning phenomenon. But, just because they come out in the morning does not mean they can't mutate into one of the many Pains that come out in the evenings, which they so often do *(see The Five Golden Rules for Pain Spotting in the Afterword)*.

SEASONAL VARIATIONS

None – the Broadsheet will be with you all year round, but just watch out for the bumper Christmas editions when there will be plenty more paper to go round.

AVOIDANCE / REVENGE STRATEGIES

1. First and foremost aim for someone who likes to read the tabloid press. These people prefer pictures to real news and it can always provide you with a diversion. The print is usually large enough to read at a distance.

2. If you find yourself attacked by the Broadsheet try tapping or knocking into their paper. Not only will this irritate them, but it will ruin their read.

3. Alternatively, if their paper is encroaching over a table and into your space, lean into it so that you head is constantly banging into it. Once again this can be assured to disturb their read.

4. Buy a broadsheet yourself – then you can have a battle of the Broadsheets. This can be great fun. And, if you want to feel superior at the same time, make sure it's the Financial Times.

5. If all else fails, get your lighter out, or if you don't smoke, a pair of scissors.

☐ Tick here when you have spotted the Broadsheet

RATE THE **BROADSHEET'S** *ANNOYANCE*

The City Boy

The City Boy is a universal hate figure. We dislike them because they earn so much from their parasitic profession. They add little value to society but extract huge fortunes. And no one sheds a tear when a City Boy gets the boot, and is positively delighted when thousands do. But it is not just because of the money they earn and the wealth they amass, it's also because they bleat when they are not getting paid even more. Court cases where an analyst has not received a ten million pound bonus when their colleagues have are all the rage. For us commuters, though, it's the way they brag about their income on the train home and conduct their business when most sane people would have stopped for the day. The Evening Standard published a wonderful piece about the City Boy some time ago. The reporter concerned had the misfortune to be travelling from Paddington to Cheltenham with a bunch of them during the Cheltenham Gold Cup race meeting. They (the City Boys) piled onto the train fully expecting to lose their shirts and have a damn good time. Here you would witness the tedious City Boy in action, shouting down their phones "Yes, yes, buy, buy, sell, sell, buy me half of Tokyo, sell me half of Manhattan." On it went, but after the race meeting they dribbled like babies as the effects of drinking too much champagne took its toll. They fooled around pushing sausages up each other's noses and into their ears. Normal behaviour for City Boys then. I'm sure that many of us have sat opposite

the odd City Boy or two. They normally inform their mates about the deals they have just made, their salary and what they are going to do with their bonarrrrse! Others have told me about City Boys who lark about on trains running up and down with their bottles of Bollinger in one hand and their bonus cheque in the other. These are extremes of course, but most City Boys can't help themselves. In the past it might have been difficult to spot the City Boy because they dressed down to blend in with the hip hop dot.com guys and girls. But now they are back to sporting their classic, thick-pinstriped suits and brogues. Other telltale signs include double-cuffed shirts, classy and sometimes quirky cufflinks and those awful padded jackets that the Toff wears. During the winter you see them wearing those extra large Barber jackets; the ones that look remarkably like a marquee.

ANNOYANCE RATING

7 – The City Boy is irritating because of their loudness and childish behaviour. They believe that because of their high-rolling income they can behave like children acting like overgrown students, lighting their farts and shouting "all right darlin'" to everyone in skirts, including Scotsmen.

RARITY

4 – The Eighties are over and long boom in decline. The heady days of barrow boys making it good in the City are fading fast. So they are less widespread than a few years ago. I used to see so many loudmouth City Boys on the train home, especially when I lived north of London, bragging about their six figure incomes and seven figure bonuses. Not any more. Sure, some still do very well, but a lot don't. In fact many of them are driving *me* around in taxis which is most gratifying. As a Pain they will not die out entirely, as the City will still survive, but they might become a little more reserved.

SEASONAL VARIATIONS

Bonus time is normally a great time to spot the City Boy. Not knowing what to do with all that extra cash, they often get totally pissed, fool around, vomit and generally misbehave. So don't be at all surprised to see a larger number of Vomiters than usual during Bonus time, which for many bankers is around March.

AVOIDANCE / REVENGE STRATEGIES

1. Keep copies of news articles heralding the latest round of job cuts in the City.

2. Ask them "How do you get hold of an City Boy after Christmas" When they reply that they don't know say "Waiter!".

3. Pose as a headhunter and ask them to contact you regarding a lucrative opportunity. When they do contact you tell them you are a fraud investigator and are looking into their financial affairs.

4. Pose as a Big Swinging Dick and shout "sell, sell, sell" down your mobile phone.

5. Take a cricket bat to their head.

☐ Tick here when you have spotted the City Boy

RATE THE
CITY BOY'S
ANNOYANCE

The Clique

The Clique breaks the mould and all the rules of rail travel. Whereas most people undertake their journey trying to avoid eye contact, conversation or any other form of engagement, the Clique is the opposite. I believe the Clique forms over time amongst people who have made the same trip for a number of years. After this length of time, people feel able to begin dialogue with those around them. A Clique is usually formed when a group of people from the same village or the same employer travel together. They will share conversations and in-jokes lost on the sane amongst us. For them it is part of their daily banter into work, but for the rest of us it is an unnecessary distraction. Perhaps they stick together because they would otherwise get beaten up. But beware pretenders. I have seen many instances of the false Clique. Here the Clique stands on the platform, coffees and teas are purchased and distributed, and then they each go their own separate ways, some to first class, some to the smokers' compartment and some to Standard Class accommodation. Don't be fooled by such platform behaviour; it's all show. A true Clique sticks together through thick and thin. A colleague of mine travels in from Winchester and observes one particular Clique in action. There are four of them and every morning they wait patiently for the complete group to arrive before they then decide on whose turn it is to buy coffees and teas. "I think it's my turn today," says one of them. "No, no, no, it's mine," says another. Eventually, having decided who is to purchase the beverages,

they move along in a tightly-coupled gang towards their usual spot on the station swapping stories of their weekends as they go. "We'll you'd never believe it, but the man next door was lying naked in the garden yesterday, I'm sure that's illegal now," "Oh I know, what is the world coming to?" "Jenny started ballet lessons on Saturday, she's a natural." And so on. When the train pulls into the platform they decide if they are going to all sit together, or if there are insufficient spaces, stand. They would rather stand together than sit apart. This is the sign of true Cliquemanship. The journey continues with this uninterrupted vacuous banter until the train reaches Waterloo. I too often travel in a carriage with a Clique. In this case, it is clear that they all work for different employers but all come in from the same town or village. The conversations are normally about the train and whether or not it is running on time. "It looks as though we are two minutes behind today." "Better than yesterday then." Laughter ensues as they all get the joke. I sit there bemused and wonder how long they have been discussing the punctuality of the train. Probably years. Are their lives so empty that this is all they have to discuss? To be reasonable, they also discuss ailments, the crossword and minor aspects of their work. But it is distracting all the same. The Clique does not accept outsiders and when a stranger enters their midst they are viewed with suspicion and ignored. They even ignore the Engager. You tend to find that the Clique will occupy the same part of the carriage every day and will save the empty seats for their friends, which is irritating if no other seats are available when you get onto the train. I imagine that when members of the Clique retire, die or are made redundant, they probably have a party and organise a plaque for them to be placed lovingly on the seat they used to occupy. In fact I wouldn't be at all surprised if they prevent anyone else from sitting on the seat until a suitable time had passed – to pay their respects.

ANNOYANCE RATING

2 – The Clique scores very low on the annoyance stakes, mainly because they are self-contained and apart from the noise of their banter present few problems to a quiet, introverted commuter such as myself.

RARITY

4 – I actually think the Clique is more common than we would like to think. I imagine that each train has between one and five Cliques on it, but considering how many other people are on the train at the same time then statistically they are pretty uncommon. I have also observed that smokers tend to be more cliquey than non-smokers. They all congregate in the buffet car, not only filling it up with ash, filth and fumes but block the thoroughfare. Laughing, joking and getting pissed night after night. I pity the poor steward who will probably die prematurely from passive smoking. If I were him, I would sue the train company.

SEASONAL VARIATIONS

There are few, if any seasonal variations in the Clique. They probably work on a longer time frame, such as the economic cycle perhaps. The Clique will ebb and flow according to the lives of its members. But, like many endangered species, they will eventually die off to be replaced by new ones. I am sure Darwin would have had a theory about this. Unfortunately I don't.

AVOIDANCE / REVENGE STRATEGIES

1. Always be wary of a group of people actively engaged in conversation.

2. Use a broadsheet paper to hide behind, but watch out for the snide comments.

3. Use your portable stereo and turn it up loud enough to drown out the noise from the banter.

4. Create your own Clique and muscle into their space. Before long we might witness gang warfare on the trains.

5. Throw a fragmentation grenade at them. One less Clique is four more seats.

☐ Tick here when you have spotted the Clique

RATE THE **CLIQUE'S** ANNOYANCE

The Creative

GENERAL CHARACTERISTICS

The Creative is an arty type and it shows. As we saw in the Preface, the Creative is someone who might be a writer, advertiser, graphic designer, actor, marketer and of course artist. I also include arts students in this category. The one thing they have in common is the flair with which they conduct themselves. They ponce around looking cool and self-important. This type of self-importance is very different from that of the Toff. Whereas the Toff will be more concerned about how superior they look to those around them, the Creative will be concerned only with themselves. They are in love with their own image and persona. They are the personification of Narcissus and to them no one else really matters. The way the Creative dresses and talks is a dead give away. Their sense of dress varies according to what they do and what stage they are at in their career, as well as how self-important they are.

For example:

Arts students tend to wear flowery, ill-fitting clothes with plenty of strong colours. Very often they will draw on their clothes in the same way young children do, although youngsters don't know any better. They will wear coloured shoes (often purple or red) and usually sport dreadlocks. They have a tendency to smell of stale sweat.

Marketers will wear all black; black shirt or black polo neck, black jacket, black shades and black shoes. For them being cool is to be the nearest thing to a black body. They may even wear black pants. Graphic designers also tend to favour all black. For them wearing the right label is so important.

Actors like to dress down these days and in fact often look rather like tramps. The only difference is that they don't beg for money (well, not often).

The Creative will talk loudly and earnestly about themselves and their achievements. Using turns of phrase such as "oh darling, you're so now" and talking as stridently as they can down the phone or to their travelling companions is the hallmark of the Creative. Recalling the chap in the Preface who spent the whole journey self-congratulating his achievement you can see why the Creative is so irritating. Then of course there are the commuters who, on spotting a celebrity will stare, point and, if they are feeling bold enough, go and seek their autograph. I am not sure what's worse, watching the smug look on the personality's face or the pathetic, hero-worshipping actions of the people falling over themselves to see them.

ANNOYANCE RATING

4 – the Creative is mildly annoying visually but more annoying to the ear. Seeing someone dressed as though they ought to be in the Mafia or wearing a pair of curtains as clothes is sufficiently out of the ordinary to distract you from whatever you are doing. But the most annoying thing about them is the way they like to talk exclusively on one subject: themselves.

RARITY

2 – Although a lot of people work in what we could consider the creative arts, you see relatively few of them on the trains. The rich and famous would rather travel by chauffeur-driven limousine than a clapped out old train. The poor arts student can't afford to travel at all. So this leaves the mid-ranking Creative such as the advertiser and marketer to bump into. Mind you, most don't get out of bed much before eleven in the morning.

SEASONAL VARIATIONS

In general there are few seasonal variations, but you might keep an eye out for the odd one or two B-list actors during the **pantomime season**.

AVOIDANCE / REVENGE STRATEGIES

1. Sit next to people who wear proper clothes such as suits.

2. Wear a colourful smock and take up as much space as you can with your exceptionally large easel.

3. Ring up a random number on your mobile and start shouting "Oh luvvie, you should have seen my latest play".

4. Pose as an art critic and discuss their latest works in a derogatory fashion using words like 'flat', and 'lacking talent'.

5. Grind up some rice and sprinkle it lightly on their lovely black jacket.

☐ Tick here when you have spotted the Creative

RATE THE
CREATIVE'S
ANNOYANCE

The Deadbeat

GENERAL CHARACTERISTICS

A lot of people like to switch off entirely during their daily commute. And although some of these are quiet they still have the ability to irritate others such as the Sleeper and Broadsheet. But there are also those who insist on making as much noise as possible. The Deadbeat falls into this category. When the Sony Walkman was launched it wasn't long before it became the must-have accessory for every youth, including myself. And although the miniaturisation of the Walkman has made it more discrete than in the past, I have recently seen some ridiculously large headphones; the sort I used to wear when undergoing a hearing test. Those who wear them look as though they should be on a beach with their metal detectors, not sitting in their pinstriped suit on the train. Quite frankly, they look like jerks. The Deadbeat will listen to the radio, CDs or tapes, but whatever they listen to you'll hear it too. Not with the same clarity of course, but enough to put you off whatever you are doing. The constant and regular beats from the music, or the faint words from a radio discussion, are enough to strain your ears in the desperate attempt to identify the band they are listening to or to catch snippets of the interview. Hiss, hiss, hiss, thud, thud, thud. Just enough to distract and not quite enough to recognise. Those who insist on using their portable stereos are not always young. Many middle-aged executives don their headphones and turn up the volume as high as it can go. Some place the radio on the rack above their heads, whilst others place it on their groin (perhaps the

vibrations give them a cheap thrill). I guess they have to turn it up so loud so as to drown out the Engager or the noise of the wheels on the track. Of course they may also be going deaf. Judging by the age of some of the users, I wouldn't be at all surprised. But unfortunately they also upset the serenity of a peaceful journey into work. One evening I was coming home and some chap was playing his radio without any headphones. He was listening to a football match with the volume turned up to maximum. I am sure everyone around him was delighted and were following every "ooh!" and "ah!" with the crowd. I, and many others, found it very off-putting. One passenger got up and told him to "turn the bloody thing down" but the man just sat there caressing the yellow radio on his lap as though it was a dog. And even to top that, I have, although only once, seen a couple of cool dudes come on the train with a huge portable stereo and proceed to play Drum and Bass music throughout the journey. As it was a weekend, I was less concerned about the noise pollution, but they looked rather comical as they tried to maintain their composure whilst looking like complete fools.

ANNOYANCE VALUE

6 – The Deadbeat will annoy anyone who is in close proximity. The annoyance will attenuate in direct proportion to the distance the Deadbeat is away from you. Perhaps there is a formula for this, maybe $Ha = 1/d^2$ where Ha is the Deadbeat's annoyance and d is the distance they are from you in metres. Science meets Pain Spotting.

RARITY

8 – The Deadbeat is surprisingly common amongst the commuting public and this, coupled with our love of gadgets, ensures they have a special place in our hearts. I look forward to a time when the portable stereo is surgically implanted into their head. Man–machine symbiosis.

SEASONAL VARIATIONS

The **summer** often brings out more Deadbeats if only because there are more students and travellers floating around. I'm afraid that both favour the use of portable stereos.

AVOIDANCE / REVENGE STRATEGIES

1. Avoid anyone who looks as though they have sprouted a set of silver ears.

2. Use some cotton wool to plug up your ears. Or, as my nephew does, earplugs.

3. Start to mouth "turn it down" repeatedly until they take off their headphones to hear what you were saying and then shout "Turn it down!" at the top of your voice.

4. Buy an inflatable hammer and repeatedly hit them on the head until they turn it off.

5. Rip the headphones from their ears and stamp on them.

☐ Tick here when you have spotted the Deadbeat

RATE THE
DEADBEAT'S
ANNOYANCE

The Death Breath

Although suffering from a blocked up nose is a miserable affair, it's often preferable to smelling the putrid breath of the person next to you. Hygiene is, of course, a personal matter but according to new research men who don't shave die younger. The theory behind this is that if you can't be bothered to shave then it is highly likely that you don't wipe your bottom properly and from this we can conclude that you don't take oral sanitation seriously either. What this means for women with facial hair or men with goatee beards, I am not sure but I don't intend to get close enough to find out. The other interesting thing about the human race is that our overall smell is loosely based on our diet. Apparently the Japanese smell of butter, the Indians of vegetables and the Europeans of carrion. The Death Breath comes in all shapes and sizes and may well coincide with other Pains and especially the Fast Fooder and Drunk. The thing about smelling other peoples' breath is that, unless you have been eating or drinking the same, your nose becomes unusually sensitive. Apart from the pungent whiff of halitosis, there is a wonderful array of aromas that find their way into your nostrils including garlic, alcohol, onion, curry, fish, smoke and of course, good old phlegm. Mornings are always a good time to assess what the Death Breath consumed the night before mainly because your nose is probably at its most sensitive. Was it a kebab, caked in chilli sauce and onions? Was it a clove of garlic? Was it a bottle of whisky? Or was it the snot from their nose? I tend to find that

onion and garlic are most common as these linger the longest. I also detect the odd aroma of smoke and surprisingly often alcohol. With respect to the Death Breath who stinks of smoke, why are they in the non-smoking carriage? They have clearly finished off their fag before getting onto the train so why don't they join their cancer-infested friends instead of breathing their stale breath over me? It's also staggering to think how many people travel to work after having a stiff one (drink I mean). I have known people who have a couple of gin and tonics before skipping off to work and judging from my colleagues' behaviour, I'm convinced most of them are alcoholics. A friend of mine loves garlic and he finds that it is a great way to secure extra space on the morning commute. He breaths very deeply in order to omit as much of the pungent fragrance around him as he can. A fog of garlic odour soon develops and envelops those around him and it isn't long before he has all the space he needs. The only people who stay next to him are Frenchmen. The evening brings out other forms of Death Breath who have been boozing it up with their associates from work, or have had their meal out. Then there are the people who must have been eating rotting flesh all day (or perhaps garbage) because their breath smells so bad I think a rat must have crawled into their mouth and died. Having someone sit next to you who reeks of booze is also horrible unless you have been drinking too. Do watch out for the Fast Fooder who polishes off their particularly large burger and then proceeds to exhale his onion breath over the person opposite. And you'll never forget the breath of the Vomiter or bulimic. This is the Death Breath at their worst.

ANNOYANCE RATING

3 – to be reasonable to the Death Breath, they are quite innocuous. Unless you are very close to them and have a particularly sensitive sense of smell they do not annoy as much as some of the other Pains. However, those who love garlic and onions are the most irritating. And don't give me the "if you eat garlic every day, you won't smell" line because I don't believe it.

RARITY

6 – with the adoption of continental and other exotic cuisines the Death Breath is becoming increasingly common especially as we seem to use garlic in every meal, including breakfast. Similarly, the rise of the messy Fast Fooder and their incumbent violently-smelling mouths helps to swell the ranks of the Death Breath.

SEASONAL VARIATIONS

Winter brings out more Death Breaths because of the prevalence of colds, flu and other illnesses. Whenever someone has this type of affliction, their mouth smells as though they have eaten a turd.

AVOIDANCE / REVENGE STRATEGIES

1. Put a cork up each of your nostrils and breathe through your mouth.

2. Carry some extra strong mints and offer them around once you sit down.

3. Use a portable fan to waft the stench away.

4. Get some of the cream that morticians use to block the smell of rotting flesh and smear it just below your nose.

5. Eat baked beans for breakfast and spend your journey passing wind.

☐ Tick here when you have spotted the Death Breath

RATE THE
DEATH BREATH'S
ANNOYANCE

The Double Seater

GENERAL CHARACTERISTICS

"Double seat, double seat, got to get a double set... double seat, double seat, got to get a double seat." This mantra pounds in your head over and over again as you weave your way through the people in the carriage. We all want space and we all want to sit alone. How many of us walk to the end of the train in the hope of finding a double seat? And when you find it, what joy, what rapture. You have no one next to you. No one invading your personal space. I love having no one around me and will deliberately seek out a seat that is on its own. The Double Seater is one of the few Pains we aspire to become, but being on the receiving end is a tad more irritating. The Double Seater, as the name suggests, will do everything they can to retain their precious extra space. Typical strategies include:

* **Leaving their case open** on the seat next to them
* **Spreading their work papers and newspapers** on the seat
* **Dropping the product of their fast food meal** all over the place, so that you would rather stand than sit next to them. Plus they stink of onions so you would have to deal with their added Death Breath
* **Having so many shopping bags and heavy cases** that there is no where else for them to go
* **Pretending to be asleep** so that you feel too embarrassed to disturb them
* **Placing their feet on the seat** next to or opposite them.

In the majority of cases these tactics seem to work as we would rather find our own space than sit next to some twerp who has all the social graces of a farmyard animal. A friend of mine told me about the Day Tripper, a variant of the Double Seater. The Day Tripper comes into the major conurbations when the train is half empty. They usually state how lovely the trains are and can't see why people make so much fuss about them. Then, on the way home, when they have bought the contents of most of the shops they visited, they not only occupy one additional seat, but often two or three. They look put out when they are asked by weary commuters to shift the junk they have purchased. Only then do they understand the true misery of commuting. I have known some commuters take the law into their own hands with the Double Seater. Some will place the offending items into the aisle or take them (without asking) and place them on the luggage racks above their heads. All they want is a seat and those who feel that they can occupy more than their fair share don't deserve any quarter. One commuter told me of a couple of Day Trippers who dumped their shopping bags on the two seats next to them and on the table. Every conceivable space was covered. As the train filled up, people would shoot them black looks and walk on. Then this angry chap got on (a Belligerent). "Excuse me are these seats taken?" "Yes, we need them for our shopping." "No you bloody well don't. I want to sit down!" "I'm sorry, but we can't find anywhere to put our bags." "Then let me help you!" This guy then proceeded to take each bag in turn and throw them onto the floor so that eventually there was enough room for him to sit down and read his paper. The women were aghast. "How dare you?!" They screamed "How dare you take up space with your crap?" came the reply, followed by "why don't you travel outside of the rush hour? You can see it's busy!" The women, realising they were not going to win the battle, assembled their shopping and ended up standing in one of the aisles for the rest of the journey. A victory for the common sense commuter.

ANNOYANCE RATING

10 – The Double Seater is very annoying indeed. What gives them the right to take more space than they have paid for? I wouldn't mind if they had purchased two tickets instead of one. Then they would have a legitimate case. But no one in their right mind would buy two tickets. So on that basis no one who commandeers an additional seat should be allowed the luxury when so many of us have to stand. And, here's some free advice for you Day Trippers out there – travel home before five o'clock.

RARITY

9 – unfortunately, the Double Seater is very common because we would all love to have that extra space to spread out. The last thing we want is someone next to us.

SEASONAL VARIATIONS

Although the Double Seater will be with you all the year around, the **summer holidays** is a fantastic time to become one yourself. With so many people on holiday, it is pure luxury. In fact the morning commute during the summer is probably as good as it gets.

You can spread out, read the biggest broadsheet paper you can find, place a picnic blanket on the table in front of you and have a veritable feast unencumbered by your fellow commuters.

AVOIDANCE / REVENGE STRATEGIES

1. Always find a double seat yourself.

2. Ask politely if the person occupying more than their allotted seat will move their bags.

3. Sit on top of the Double Seater's baggage.

4. If you can, throw the Double Seater's bags out of an open window.

5. Scream, shout and jump up and down like a spoilt child.

☐ Tick here when you have spotted the Double Seater

*RATE THE **DOUBLE SEATER'S** ANNOYANCE*

The Drunk

GENERAL CHARACTERISTICS

The Drunk is the antecedent of the Vomiter and shares many of the characteristics of the Engager. Drunks come in singles or groups, with groups posing the greatest threat of disruption.

One of the biggest problems with the Drunk is that they lose their self control in respect of their:

- **Tongues** – they will spurt out an incredible amount of inarticulate rubbish when they have had too much alcohol
- **Bodily functions** – yes they will
- **Emotions** – many Drunks have the tendency to turn both soppy and violent.

The Drunk engages those around him because his ability to restrain conversation goes with the third bottle of wine. At this point they rapidly turn into the Engager, albeit a Drunk one. Because they are drunk they make no sense whatsoever as their words blend into one long stream of nothingness. I was told of one story that related to the Drunk. Going home one evening, the unsuspecting commuter was searching for a space in the otherwise overcrowded train. What luck, he found what seemed to be a part-empty carriage with some spare seats in it. As he made his way towards them he couldn't help but notice that the remainder of coach was

packed. No matter, on he went until he reached the vacant seats. Then he realised why they were empty. In front of him was a drunk but not just the usual sort of drunk, worse for wear and loudmouthed. This one had managed to wet himself. His trousers were dark with the product of his bladder. The seat was sodden and the floor was awash with his bitter-smelling urine. He, of course, was oblivious. The commuter beat a hasty retreat and cowered with the remaining passengers. Over the course of the journey the liquid gradually made its way along the carriage much to the delight of all and sundry. A colleague also experienced some of the more extreme of the Drunk's behaviour. He was standing by the door of the train waiting to get off at the end of the journey when a man tried to push past him. As there was nowhere for this chap to go, he stood his ground. The man behind kept sighing and muttering under his breath "w****r, w****r." My colleague could smell the familiar scent of cider on his breath as he got off the train and walked along the platform. The Drunk was walking right behind him clipping his heels with the tips of his shoes. After a minute or so of this behaviour my colleague turned around and said "What's your problem?" "You are!" came the reply. "So, do you want to make something of it?" As my colleague was ex-army he felt able to handle this man. In fact the Drunk was almost half his size. "OK, right here, right now!" "Oh no, not here," replied the Drunk. "There are too many police around". They went outside. "Right," said the Drunk, "you go first." "What do you mean I go first?" replied my colleague. The Drunk, realising he stood no chance, ran off.

ANNOYANCE RATING
7 – the Drunk is undoubtedly annoying for a variety of reasons. First, because of the smell of alcohol on their breath. Second, because the alcohol loosens their tongues. Third, because they don't know when to stop. And finally because they lose control of their bodily functions.

RARITY
5 – the Drunk is pretty common and is a reflection on people's need to escape their daily lives by turning to the bottle. Single Drunks are generally more common than groups, although groups can be spotted surprisingly often and chiefly at certain times of the year.

SEASONAL VARIATIONS
You will certainly glimpse more over the **Christmas and New Year** periods as this is when most people let their hair down and go a little mad particularly with the booze. You will also notice more during the football season when supporters of the winning and losing teams will do their utmost to drink every bar dry and will usually travel home exceptionally drunk. The same can be said of cricket fans travelling home after a long day in the sun and copious amounts of liquid refreshment.

AVOIDANCE / REVENGE STRATEGIES
1. Always travel during daylight hours.

2. Study the sporting calendar so you can avoid the group of drunk supporters and avoid the usual festive seasons.

3. Offer them the telephone number for Alcoholics Anonymous.

4. Pour a drink over their head and tell them the drinks are on them.

5. Shake a can of Special Brew for five minutes then offer it to the Drunk as you leave the train. Watch from the platform as he unwittingly sprays himself and the rest of the carriage with its contents.

☐ Tick here when you have spotted the Drunk

RATE THE
DRUNK'S
ANNOYANCE

The Engager

GENERAL CHARACTERISTICS

You have had a hard day at work, people have annoyed you, hassled you and generally pissed you off. You wouldn't choose to top this off with a long commute home but you have no option. All you want to do is retreat into a protective bubble and read the latest bestselling novel or evening newspaper (preferably not a Broadsheet) and drink your well-earned gin and tonic. The people around you seem quite normal and it looks as though you will have a peaceful trip home. Then someone begins to engage in mindless dialogue with you and the people next to you. "What's your name?" "What do you do for a living?" "I'm off to see my sick aunt", "I can't believe what Tony Blair is doing to the country, can you?" or "What about the economy, do you think it will ever recover?" Yes, it's the Engager. The Engager is typified by a unique ability to spew out a continuous stream of trivia, intrusive questions and pointless dialogue. In fact they barely draw breath and are the human equivalent of a bagpipe. And, although everyone is doing their best to avoid eye contact (a red rag to a bull for the Engager) they are undeterred. They will continue until they catch someone acknowledging their presence. Then it's too late, as they will become more personal, sharing their deepest problems and seeking out yours. In extreme cases they ask if you would like to share their drink and food. Worse still, they ask if they can eat your food! They won't stop for the entire journey. Everyone is undoubtedly thinking "Sod off!", but of course no one ever says so for fear of being ensnared,

plus it's terribly un-British. Although you pray that the Engager will be getting off at the first stop, you can bet your bottom dollar that they will be going right to the end of the line. Observing others who get collared by the Engager is always amusing; they squirm and shift in their seats, trying to avoid eye contact or displaying any sign that they might have acknowledged the Engager's presence. If they commence dialogue with the Engager, it is with disdain and disinterest, but this is never enough to perturb the Engager as even the slightest signal is enough to spur them on. Some people might move away, but this is always followed by an incredulous "Don't go!"; "Look at that miserable git," or "Go and sit somewhere else then!" It's as though they are the ones that have been offended. A friend of mine told me of a lady who was pestered by an Engager whilst proofreading a document. "What are you working on?" he said. "I've work to do and no time to chat!" came the frosty reply. This was the come-on he wanted. He continued to engage the poor lady. She told him a number of times that if he persisted she would move. Eventually she did. The more fortunate reach their stop, or pretend to be busy working or even feign sleep – though working often provokes some comment such as "Pretending to work then?" People leaving the train or those who do not rise to the tirade of questions is the cue for the Engager to seek out their next victim, perhaps on the other side of the aisle. I recently shared a journey home with a bunch of software engineers who were the worse for wear after a day out on the town. Two of the women insisted on asking inane questions to everyone around them and were sufficiently loud to annoy the entire carriage. One fellow passenger moved – to the usual "Don't go". The guy opposite was hassled throughout the entire commute by these two stupid women who insisted he looked just like Russell Crowe (which of course he didn't – in fact he looked more like Ella Fitzgerald).

ANNOYANCE RATING

10 – few people really want to get involved with the Engager, so their annoyance rating is usually very high. But they just don't get it; they persist and will continue to quiz you about your job, your life, in fact about anything until you give in and strike up a conversation.

RARITY

3 – Thankfully, the Engager is quite rare, as most people are just too knackered or disinterested to talk to anyone (apart from, of course, someone at the end of their mobile phone). The only exception to this is when a train breaks down. Then, for some strange reason, everyone starts to engage with everyone else. A bit of the Blitz Sprit creeping in perhaps. The Engager's rarity decreases the later you go home, so my advice is leave for home early if you want to avoid them. If you leave it too late you might also bump (or perhaps slip) into the Vomiter.

SEASONAL VARIATIONS

Any **party season** tends to bring out more Engagers than the norm, as they are often closely related to a mild form of the Drunk. In particular, **Christmas** is a great time to spot the Engager, dressed in tuxedos, wearing flashing Santa hats, or just generally worse for wear after the Christmas party.

AVOIDANCE / REVENGE STRATEGIES

1. Always carry a broadsheet paper with you. When you spot the Engager, whip it out and hide behind it.

2. Keep your head down and pretend you're deaf or an overseas visitor.

3. Use your mobile phone to ring someone and engage in a long conversation about the painful people you meet on train journeys.

4. Start picking your nose and flicking it at them.

5. Resort to physical violence.

☐ Tick here when you have spotted the Engager

RATE THE
ENGAGER'S
ANNOYANCE

The Enquirer

GENERAL CHARACTERISTICS

Many people find train travel bemusing – and not just tourists. Those who do not travel frequently have a need to develop their plans interactively through exhaustive conversations at the ticket office or with any other train company staff they encounter. The problem is that for regular commuters, familiar with the nuances and idiosyncrasies of travelling by train, the Enquirer is a real pain. Enquirers tend to appear during the mornings as you are queuing for your ticket. You've been doing the same trip so long that you have the routine down to a T with still time to make the train. This works well if you are purchasing a daily or weekly ticket and as long as everyone else is. But life is not always so simple. Problems start when those in front are paying for, or enquiring about, something more complex than you bargained for. Types of Enquirer include:

- those who choose to **renew their annual season ticket on a weekday morning**
- people who start to **ask inane questions about car parking** and how much it costs for every conceivable permutation
- **retired folk** who now have the time to practise rapport-building by engaging in pointless conversations that have nothing to do with the purchase of tickets
- **belligerents who want to complain** about the punctuality and general disrepair of the trains

- **travellers who wish to find the cheapest deal** before committing to payment
- **frustrated commuters** who attempted to buy their tickets over the Internet only to find that they haven't arrived
- those whose **annual season tickets no longer work** in automatic gates because of software upgrades.

Many of these involve the ticket office staff thumbing through timetables, discussing pricing options and routes, and holding up the ever-lengthening queue of commuters who know they have only another 30 seconds before their train leaves. A number of enquiries involve the customer completing forms, slowly and with total disregard for the log jam being created behind them. They should, of course, step aside as they complete the document thereby allowing the next person to get their ticket, but now they have their place they don't want to be bumped to the back of the line, and inevitably want to ask more questions about the form to ensure none of those in the queue catch their train. I have heard conversations such as "I was wondering, if I want to travel to Edinburgh which is the best route? Should I go cross country, or is it best to go into London and then back out?" and "Whilst here, could you tell me the costs of a return to Manchester travelling out on Tuesday, returning next Saturday with a Young Person's Railcard?" Valuable minutes are wasted as the guy the other side of the counter attempts to service the current customer's needs, with impassive glances to assess the state of annoyance of those behind the jerk he is serving. I wouldn't envy him his job. What they seem to do is zone in on the current person to try and block out the palpable fury of those behind so they don't disturb their karma – the queue is the system, it's not their system.

ANNOYANCE RATING

8 – The Enquirer always rates highly in terms of annoyance. You only have to see the daggers being shot at them by other people in the queue. Why can't they restrict their questions to after the morning rush when they can take as long as they like? Also, why don't they use other forms of information gathering like the Web, the telephone, even the printed timetables that are stationed all around the building? The Lord only knows.

RARITY

9 – The Enquirer is very common because of the vast array of questions they could ask. It's an Enquirer's charter. So I'm afraid there will always be someone in front of you who insists on making an enquiry and it is sod's law that this will be when you are in a tearing hurry to make your train.

SEASONAL VARIATIONS

Summer will bring out more Enquirers than at any other time. This is when you get more day trippers asking about the offers available and discussing routes and options.

AVOIDANCE / REVENGE STRATEGIES

1. Always buy your tickets at the end of the day.

2. If you have a credit card use the automatic ticket machines (assuming they are working, of course).

3. Attempt to jump the queue by feigning an emergency.

4. Push forward so that the Enquirer is shoved aside and ideally falls over, then blame it on the person behind you.

5. Start a slow hand clap with the rest of the queue and begin to chant "Why are we waiting?".

☐ Tick here when you have spotted the Enquirer

RATE THE
ENQUIRER'S
ANNOYANCE

The Family

I have nothing against families you understand; I have one myself. But they should never be allowed on trains, during peak hours or at all. Families come in all shapes and sizes, but share a number of especially annoying characteristics, including:

- **Unruliness**
- **Loudness**
- **Disorganisation**
- **Untidiness**
- **Disrespect**

As we know, most families are dysfunctional so we shouldn't be too surprised by their behaviour on trains. Let's face it, we all look down our noses at the behaviours of children and their parents, whether in the supermarket (the kids are screaming, throwing tantrums and rolling about on the floor), around town (ditto), in restaurants (they can't even hold a knife and fork and usually refuse to eat anything. A product of too many TV dinners and career women not bothering to bring up their kids properly). In fact anywhere. But their behaviour is amplified when it is confined within a train carriage. Coming home one evening I met a toff family – you know the type, parents who couldn't spell parenting, let alone

practise it. They consisted of a boy of about eleven or twelve, a girl about nine or ten and their errant, and totally incompetent, father. The boy was eating his McDonald's meal (thereby qualifying as an instant Fast fooder, spilling chips, burgers and drink everywhere). Worse, he couldn't be bothered to dispose of his trash (or himself, for that matter) in a responsible manner, kicking the bag and remains of the 'meal' under the table to the man opposite – who naturally kept kicking it back. Dad was, of course, oblivious to the mess or his idiot son's bloody-mindedness. Not content with the mess he had made, the brat had to do all he could to grab the attention of his unresponsive father. "Dad, I want your coffee – I always have coffee at home." "Dad, are you claustrophobic?" "Dad, can I borrow your mobile phone?" "Dad, is my ticket valid?" (The ticket inspector had just punched it.) "Dad, what year were you born?" Dad was ignoring them – God knows how, the constant pestering would drive anyone else from the carriage if they didn't throw the brats out of the window first. Then we have the Interactive Parent. These are the parents who engage with their children about everything going on inside and outside the train, in a distinctive middle-class, quasi-educational tone that embraces the whole compartment. "Mummy, Mummy, why is the train slowing down?" Answer: "Well, darling, the driver-man is putting on the brakes because we're coming into the station, and you know what the brakes are, don't you… the station is where they join two trains together so only one engine has to pull us all the way to London… now, what did we learn last week about engines?" …and on, and on, and bloody on! Why do they have to turn everything into an educational experience when most of their offspring will be flipping burgers ten years from now? Oh, Ollie, you have turned out to be such a disappointment after all those school fees. Then there are the parents (or nannies) who insist on reading out aloud to their charges. It might be wonderful for the beautiful little boy or girl, but it is pure agony for the rest of us.

ANNOYANCE RATING

9 – families are loud, annoying and poorly behaved. But it is quite strange how train journeys seem to affect children. Even my bunch, usually well-behaved, go off the rails when on the rails, so to speak. At least I restrict my family travel to weekends, when the carriages are so littered with unruly children that no one will notice.

RARITY

4 – Thankfully, the Family does not come out that often, as they are restricted by childminding, otherwise known as the educational system. But when they do, they make up for it in spades.

SEASONAL VARIATIONS

School holidays are a great time to spot the Family. So if you are really looking for unadulterated misery choose your journey so that it coincides with when the kids are out of their daily drudge and into yours. But if you want to go the whole hog, opt for the summer or winter holidays, as the Family is normally accompanied by abundant luggage and skiing equipment which they strive to

keep next to them either on their seats or blocking the aisles (see the Traveller). Try and see anyone get past a huge Delsey case – nigh on impossible. But the Family doesn't care; it is merely doing what comes naturally – being dysfunctional.

AVOIDANCE / REVENGE STRATEGIES

1. Work from home during school holidays.

2. Upgrade to first class.

3. Get the extra early train – even families don't get up that early.

4. Lobby your local MP to see if he will support a bill to prevent families from travelling on busy commuter routes.

5. Stick your fingers down your throat and vomit over the children.

☐ Tick here when you have spotted the Family

RATE THE
FAMILY'S
ANNOYANCE

The Fast Fooder

GENERAL CHARACTERISTICS

We love fast food. Whether it is a kebab, McDonald's, Burger King or Pizza, few of us can resist its appeal. Shoving down that double cheese burger and fries whilst on the move is particularly gratifying as it saves you having to cook and wash up. There are, however, three problems this presents to the average commuter:

The mess. Dealing with the detritus which consists of globules of mayonnaise, half-eaten burgers, chips, cabbage and chilli sauce is no fun. This presents a problem to those who eat it as well as those who find their beautiful dress or Armani suit caked in the product of someone else's meal. But the real question is what to do with the debris? There are few bins, so the majority ends up spilt on the tables, stuck to the seats and littering the floor.

The stench. For those who are not eating it is pure torture, either because they know they have got some rancid excuse of a meal waiting for them at home, they cannot be bothered to cook, or because they have just eaten some wonderful cuisine from a Gordon Ramsey restaurant and the prospect of eating anything else makes them want to vomit, especially if it happens to be a bacon double cheeseburger.

The view. The spectacle of watching someone make light work of a burger, kebab, pizza or whatever culinary delight they have purchased from the station concourse is a visual affront. But it is not just watching them masticate with their mouths open that is so disgusting, it's the way the various condiments and fat ooze down their chins (yes, I do mean chins) and onto their clothes. I do not believe it is possible to eat fast food without making a God-awful mess.

You can spot a regular Fast Fooder from the stains on their clothes: the off-white from the mayonnaise, the creamy orange from the thousand island dressing and the blood red blobs from the tomato sauce. Regular Fast Fooders feast off all sorts of stuff, some of which is more noisy and messy than the rest. They are normally untidy, smelly and leave a trail of filth wherever they go. They never clean up after themselves and they probably live in rented accommodation with excrement on the walls. What I particularly hate is the mess they leave. How many times have I walked onto a train only to find the seats covered in cabbage from a kebab, or mayo smeared all over the table which is swimming in a pool of sticky Coke? Young Fast Fooders are no better, and can be a lot worse. They are more likely to throw their food around even when travelling with their parents. They certainly do not clear up after themselves (see The Family). Whenever I see a Fast Fooder, or the by-product of their favourite meal, my usual reaction is to pass it by in the hope of finding a more suitable seat. All too often however, there is an entire suite of seats and tables piled high with the wreckage of other peoples' banquets or a succession of Mammoths piling into their third meal of the evening. One of my colleagues was coming to work recently only to have the guy next to him eating a Pot Noodle. Surely that is taking it just a bit too far. I mean, having toast and coffee at seven o'clock, but a Pot Noodle?

ANNOYANCE RATING

4 to 7 – This will vary depending on a number of factors, including how hungry you are, whether you are looking forward to a slap up meal at home, or whether you are just plain envious. But I believe it is the smell that is probably the most annoying aspect because it has the tendency to make you feel slightly nauseous. With no air conditioning you can't escape the stench and, unlike the Phantom Farter, the smell tends to linger.

RARITY

8 – The Fast Fooder will come out at any time during the day, although they will be more concentrated around mealtimes. For the Pain Spotter however, the best time to see them is at the end of the day, although as we saw above, they can occasionally appear in the morning. I believe the Fast Fooder will become increasingly common as more of us are divorced, remain single and the art of cooking dies out despite the efforts of Delia Smith. I know one or two people who already survive off fast food as their staple diet.

SEASONAL VARIATIONS
None.

AVOIDANCE / REVENGE STRATEGIES
1. Always travel between meals.

2. Carry a dustpan and brush with you so that you can clear up the mess when you get onto the train.

3. Leave a copy of *Fast Food Nation* lying around in the hope that it might change their dietary habits.

4. Engage the Fast Fooder in a debate about the evils of fast food and what it does to their body.

5. Simulate a coughing fit in which the contents of your lungs find their way onto the Fast Fooder's burger.

☐ Tick here when you have spotted the Fast Fooder

RATE THE
FAST FOODER'S
ANNOYANCE

The Flamboyant Groin

GENERAL CHARACTERISTICS

The Flamboyant Groin is a Pain that is primarily restricted to the male of the species. As in nature their higher brain is incapable of overriding the primitive compulsion to display their genitalia to potential mates. This is the chap who sits next to you with legs at ninety degrees so his knee is in your territory and thigh pressed against yours, pushing hard to ensure his groin is on full display and leaving you with little or no room for manoeuvre. This can be significantly more distressing when he's opposite you, because of the flagrancy of his genital display. If he's wearing shorts it can be worse still; when they are not wearing underwear, you can get a lot more than you bargained for. It's worse than someone wearing white swimming trunks in the pool – nothing is left to the imagination. From Chipolata to Cumberland you see them all. When the Flamboyant Groin is sitting next to you, you have to tilt your body away and press your knees together so the more macho he becomes the more like a prim librarian you look. One lady traveller told me how she spent a long hot journey watching the gentleman opposite not only spread his legs as far apart as was humanly possible, but then proceeded to scratch and fondle his genitals for most of the journey. She said it was disgusting. If she really wanted to see some man play with his one-eyed trouser snake she would watch a pornographic movie. Let's face it, when you are thinking about work, the last thing on your mind is pocket billiards.

The lady concerned asked that the gentlemen close his legs; he said nothing, winked and opened his legs that little bit further. He was obviously a skilled practioner of Yoga. I often sit next to a man on my train who combines the smug behaviour of the Broadsheet with the uncalled-for actions of the Flamboyant Groin. Not satisfied with taking up all the space above waist height, he wants to commandeer every inch below the waist too. I rarely give up without a fight and will push my legs apart so that he is crushed up against the side of the train. It often turns out to be a battle of wills but the feeling of having my hot thigh against his is sufficiently disconcerting for him to back down. We might of course behave very differently if it was a woman who was being flamboyant with her groin. Somehow, I don't think most men would be offended at the deliberate display and may well choose to sit opposite them. But that's enough of that.

ANNOYANCE RATING

4 – In general, the Flamboyant Groin is more annoying to women passengers than men, although the effects of spreading ones legs in a confined space is always going to cause irritation. I think the only thing worse than this is to have a combination of the Mammoth, Broadsheet and the Flamboyant Groin. That would be really unbearable.

RARITY

6 – With so little legroom on the train and the macho behaviour of men, the Flamboyant Groin is not as rare as you might think. Furthermore, with the Human Race gradually increasing in height, it is likely that we will see more of this Pain over time.

SEASONAL VARIATIONS

Although the Flamboyant Groin is with us **throughout the year**, the visual impact of their performance deteriorates with the onset of Summer. This is due to a combination of factors. First, people tend to dress down during the warmer months. Second, you tend to get a lot more tourists

who often wear ill-fitting shorts. And, finally, the sap is rising.

AVOIDANCE / REVENGE STRATEGIES

1. Always sit on seats facing the same direction as those in front. At least you won't be getting an eyeful.

2. Place your case next to you on the floor, thereby restricting the movements of your travelling companion.

3. Take a digital photograph of the groin on display and add it to your Flamboyant Groin website's members-only lounge.

4. Take a pair of nutcrackers with you and throw them from side to side in a threatening manner. You might also like to crack a couple of walnuts.

5. Use a water pistol to spray the groin area of the Flamboyant Groin so it looks as though they have wet themselves.

☐ Tick here when you have spotted the Flamboyant Groin

RATE THE **FLAMBOYANT GROIN'S** ANNOYANCE

The Gadget

Every aspect of our life is impacted by technology in one shape or form and none so more than work. There are now a wealth of contraptions available which keep us in touch with our office, our friends and help us lead more successful and enjoyable existences. Yeah, right! As far as I'm concerned the only people who believe such marketing claptrap are the men and women who must have the leading edge of technology in their hands (or pockets). I call such people the Gadget: you know, the sort of person who must have the latest gizmo even though it has no value whatsoever and in all likelihood doesn't work properly. In fact I think the Gadget is someone who could benefit from having Batman's utility belt if only because it would provide the opportunity to store a gadget for every conceivable use. And, boy, are there gadgets, including mobile phones, laptop computers, MP3 players, personal digital assistants (PDAs), wireless email devices, pagers – and so on. If possible the Gadget will have them all and will usually sport the latest model in order to feel superior to any other Gadget who happens to be watching. I watched one commuter on the way in one morning take his PDA out of its rather lovely velvet case and caress it gently. You could see the love in the man's eyes as he stared fondly at the blue screen. After fiddling with it, he placed it carefully back in its case and slipped it back into his pocket. He then got his mobile phone out, turned it on, checked if he had received any messages and then turned it off. Then he got his PDA out again, fondled it,

turned it on, switched it off and placed it back into his pocket. He finally got out a radio out and plugged himself in. He was also very fat and was munching his way through some fast food. And I am sure there was a bulge in his trousers. It's rare that you can spot the Mammoth, Fast Fooder, Pervert and Gadget all at once (look at Golden Rule number 2 in the Afterword – don't stereotype). The Gadget will often get into deep intellectual and, at times, animated conversations with fellow Gadgets about the relative merits of their devices. On one occasion a friend watched two men showing off the functionality of their mobile phones. This was when mobiles were in their infancy and people would kneel before anyone who had one. These two chaps were so excited they were beside themselves "Well my phone can store the names and numbers of twenty people!" "Ah, but mine has some cool games on it!" Why on earth would you want to play games on a screen no bigger than a match box? With mobile phones now allowing you to watch movies and surf the net, the opticians must be looking forward to lots of business in near future as a troop of Gadgets end up with severe eye problems. Another form of the Gadget is the Techno-boy. These are the people who talk in gobbledegook about white hot technology. They usually shout, are often unkempt and get very, very excited, often foaming at the mouth. Most of what they say is wrapped up in the world of techno-speak which means nothing to anyone but them. Typical topics of conversation include the technical compositions of their laptops, from how much memory they have to what programs they are running. The important thing to recognise is that the Gadget is not restricted to the younger generation. Many in their late middle-age and increasingly in old-age become almost obsessive about their Gadgets; it's as though they want to make up for lost time. They will wax lyrical about how wonderful their gadgets are and how they have transformed their lives. What sort of life did they have before it was transformed by the latest technology? One can only wonder.

ANNOYANCE RATING

4 – most of the time the Gadget is mildly annoying, as they only tend to distract you with their rapid hand movements (funnily enough, most of these take place in their groin which is a little disconcerting) rather than annoy with noise or conversation. I do make an exception for those Gadgets who use their PDAs. For me they rate as a 7.

RARITY

6 – The Gadget is gradually increasing in numbers as more and more technology reaches the market. Soon their briefcases will be stuffed full with all the gear of modern living and there will be no more room for their tired-looking sandwiches.

SEASONAL VARIATIONS

Gadgets do not follow any normal seasonal behaviour as their lives are governed by the release of new technology. And with suppliers of technology desperately trying to flog the latest in senseless labour-saving devices you are bound to spot the Gadget sooner or later. And what you notice is that these contraptions get more and more stupid. One of my friends pointed out to me the latest in mobile telephony. It looks like a huge plastic ear that fits around your lughole which allows you to walk about and take incoming calls in a casual and nonchalant way.

AVOIDANCE / REVENGE STRATEGIES

1. Always sit next to an old age pensioner – they tend to be gadget free.

2. Import the latest gadget from Japan and walk up and down the carriage showing it off.

3. Write to your train operating company and ask if they could have a gadget-free carriage.

4. Fix a very strong electromagnetic device inside your shoe and use it to jam all the Gadget's toys in your carriage.

5. Take a phial of sulphuric acid, pour it over their gadget and watch it melt before your eyes.

☐ Tick here when you have spotted the Gadget

RATE THE **GADGET'S** ANNOYANCE

The Gaggle

GENERAL CHARACTERISTICS

The Gaggle usually comprises a group of women who are not frequent enough commuters to be classified as a Clique. The Gaggle, as the name suggests, is a group of women who jaw, and jaw, and jaw. In fact I don't believe they ever stop and they certainly seem to be able to talk non-stop without drawing breath. I reckon they walk around with an aqualung permanently attached to their respiratory system. They will talk about anything and everything. Topics range from the weather, their children and how talented, special and gifted they are, to what they did yesterday and what they intend to do tomorrow. Whatever they talk about it will be in infinite detail. No aspect remains untold. Minutiae is their business. The Gaggle is often known as the Life Repeater as they will repeat every aspect of their life through the same stories, anecdotes and yarns. The Gaggle demonstrates the fundamental differences between the sexes. Whereas men rarely have much more than a short and often work-based conversation, women are much more socially aware and communicative. It is well known that those parts of our brain that deal with communication are significantly larger in women than men. This is why the Gaggle is predominantly a female Pain. Enough physiology for now. I was travelling into work a few years ago when I happened to come across one of my first Gaggles. This one was a writing circle who, I deduced, wrote for women's magazines. "My short story for Woman's Own was published last week." "That's wonderful, Kay, what was it all about?" "Oh, about this child who was abducted by

her estranged father..." This and the many other stories that followed covered similar ground and had plenty of "Oh I know"s and "Well I never"s peppered throughout. I was totally distracted. I could not concentrate on anything but their twittering. Other commuters have told me of similar stories of women travelling together. Many have told me of the women shoppers who, having occupied most of the space around them with a zillion plastic bags full of their *wonderful* purchases, recall their day in immense detail, the shops they visited, the characteristics of each and every shop assistant, the process of selecting their chosen purchases and how their feet ache. Then, not satisfied with boring everyone in the compartment, they ring up the members of their Gaggle who were unable to join them and repeat the complete conversation. Not only does the person on the other end of the phone understand what they missed, but we can get a second and third helping. What is truly amazing is that they repeat the tale word perfect. That's without the two women who sit opposite each other, rather than next to each other, in order that the rest of the carriage can share their inane conversation (whose rules are that silence must be avoided at all costs no matter how meaningless and repetitious the content).

ANNOYANCE RATING

8 – The problem with the Gaggle is that their incessant chitchat is a constant distraction. Trying to concentrate on anything but their talking is impossible because you can't help but to tune into their ridiculous discussions. And because they do not stop you have no possibility of any respite until you get off the train.

RARITY

2 – despite there being more women than men, the Gaggle is still pretty rare. Maybe it is because there are more working women than there used to be. However, as women live longer we should expect to see more of the Gaggle, especially as Baby Boomers retire and figure out what to do with the rest of their lives.

SEASONAL VARIATIONS

The Gaggle tends to be more visible during the **spring** and **summer** months when the weather is fine and they feel like having a girls' day out. The conference season also tends to bring out more Gaggles, although here you might find more work- related ones. With meetings that focus exclusively on women in the workplace such as "Women in IT", "Busygirl forums" and such like, you are bound to listen in on some great conversations.

AVOIDANCE / REVENGE STRATEGIES

1. Sit next to men. As long as they are not displaying any of the other irritating commuting habits, you should be in for a quiet journey.

2. Pour acid in your ears.

3. Pop a baby's dummy into each of the Gaggle's mouths.

4. Pose as the Verbal Diarrhoea Police and issue each Gaggle member with an on-the-spot fine for talking so much drivel,

5. Use a white noise generator to drown out their row.

☐ Tick here when you have spotted the Gaggle

RATE THE
GAGGLE'S
ANNOYANCE

The Group

GENERAL CHARACTERISTICS

We have seen the Clique and the Gaggle. Now it's the turn of the Group. The Group, like the Gaggle but unlike the Clique, is an infrequent user of the trains. The most important thing to remember when looking out for the Group is that they are off duty. What I mean by this is that they are out of their normal work-based context which gives them permission to behave very differently from the norms established during their daily routine. The Group can consist of:

- **Work colleagues** who have attended a training programme
- **A bunch of strangers** who have met at a conference and feel the intense desire to network
- **A group of friends** who have had a day out together
- **More than one family** combining an outing
- **Sports fans** attending a football, rugby or cricket match
- **School children** on a day out.

All share the same characteristics. They all tend to talk incessantly, speak in incredibly loud voices and drink vast amounts of booze (apart from the school children who just spill theirs). They are experts at stating the bleedin' obvious as well and will often come out with such statements as "Oh, I can't believe why

anyone would want to make this journey every day. It's so tiring." Yes, love, we would dearly not have to take the same journey day in and day out, I can assure you. The school children usually requisition at least half a carriage and spend their time running up and down, talking about boys (or girls) and generally making far too much noise. Their incompetent teachers are incapable of controlling them and resign themselves to getting quietly drunk with their colleagues. So much for the adage that a child should be seen and not heard. I recently shared a carriage with some loud academic archaeologists. Now this is incredibly rare. Not only were they unnecessarily loud despite being barely twelve inches apart from each other, they went on, and on, and on, and on, about their archaeological digs. "Yes, we have at least three breakfasts a day and the beer is so warm. But don't drink the local form of Stella, it's not the same." The conversation covered such topics as Egyptians sleeping on the floor, malaria, sleeping arrangements as well as student life which inevitably dwelled upon the nubile students. (These were a bunch of academics in their late twenties or early thirties who had never quite grown up or indeed felt able to earn a proper living. This reminds me of the maxim "Those who can, do. Those who can't teach, and those who can't teach, teach teachers".) This group seemed to combine the worst attributes of the Social Climber (of course, impossible on an academic's salary), Gaggle and Traveller. But it was the combination of their hip hop, hipity hop trendy attitudes and language which was so utterly boring, this and their intellectual masturbation. What lies at the heart of the Group's ability to irritate is that they have no idea of the conventions surrounding train travel.

ANNOYANCE VALUE
6 – the Group is annoying because they are loud and raucous; something that is totally unacceptable.

RARITY
5 – The Group is quite rare but unfortunately not rare enough. It is surprising how many Groups you see. Workers sharing the same training course appear to be the most common and groups of families the most rare.

SEASONAL VARIATIONS
You will see the Group in its various guises **all year round**. You will generally spot groups of school children during term time when they are on their obligatory museum trips, but do watch out for the summer field trips. Groups of football and rugby supporters will be restricted to their respective seasons and groups of workers on training courses will follow the economic cycle. Of all Pains, this is the hardest to keep track of.

AVOIDANCE / REVENGE STRATEGIES
1. Sit as far as you can away from the Group as possible.

2. Wear a Hannibal Lector face mask. This is especially useful when dealing with a bunch of school children.

3. Have a number of "No Groups Please" signs made up and place them throughout the carriage.

4. Enlist a couple of commuters and tie the Group up using a combination of strong twine and duct tape.

5. Pose as an environmental health officer and use a decibel meter to test how loud they are and then threaten to prosecute them under the Noise Abatement Act.

☐ Tick here when you have spotted the Group

RATE THE **GROUP'S** ANNOYANCE

The Hero

The Hero deserves some particular attention as a Pain. Like the Stinker, they tend to appear en masse at particular times of the year, but unlike the Stinker, whose sweet odour comes out only during the summer months, the Hero can appear at other times as well. The Hero is someone who fundamentally believes in the Protestant work ethic (thank you, Martin Luther) and the importance of soldiering on even when they are at death's door. Although they might believe they are doing their company a great service by demonstrating their commitment, I'm afraid they are not. And we, the commuting public, do not appreciate it. There is nothing quite so disgusting as sitting next to someone or, God forbid, opposite, as they sneeze without a handkerchief. Although you might attempt to avoid the globules of phlegm as they accelerate towards you faster than a speeding car, before you know it you have lumps of congealed yellow snot over your lapels, trousers and face. Then there is the person who constantly sniffs, desperately trying to reacquaint the clear liquid emanating from their nostrils with the inside of their nose as it cascades over their lips. And, we must not forget the person who is constantly clearing their throat in the effort to dislodge that particularly stubborn lump of unmentionable substance from their lungs. One colleague was on a lengthy rail journey some time ago during which he had the luck to sit opposite a Hero. Every minute or so the man opposite would sniff, bring the phlegm into his mouth and then gulp the bolus of snot down with immense

gusto. After 30 minutes of this, my friend jumped up, went to the buffet car, retrieved some napkins, walked calmly back and thrust them into the hands of the man opposite. "Can I suggest you use these, as I have had enough of your antics," he said. The man looked incredulous, thinking he was dealing with his illness rather well, but used the tissues all the same. Unfortunately my colleague then had to spend the next hour watching him use the tissues to pick lumps out of his nose and inspect them. I have witnessed people use their newspapers as makeshift hankies, leaving the sodden results of their efforts on the seats once they have finished. I have even seen people use their shirt sleeves. Now, I fully expect my son to do this, but a forty year old? Why doesn't the Hero go home and suffer elsewhere rather than bringing their germs and filth to everyone else? Let's face it, their employer doesn't want to see them, so why should we? There is one other Hero who is closely related to the Vomiter. However, unlike the Vomiter whose predicament is created by alcohol and substance abuse, the Hero Vomiter is someone who is genuinely ill. Unfortunately being stuck on a packed train is the last place they ought to be and judging by the results, I'm sure everyone else feels the same. One person I know was feeling particularly unwell whilst travelling on the Tube. The carriage was packed and she had no receptacle in which to chunder. This was unfortunate for the young men standing next to her because when she did throw up it went all over their lower legs and feet. Apparently you could see the chunky vegetable soup she had consumed earlier. Having struggled off the train at Kings Cross, she was then sick all over the platform. What's interesting is that throughout no one made an effort to see if she was OK. I guess they assumed she was drunk.

ANNOYANCE RATING
10 – I'm afraid there is nothing quite so irritating as having some fool coughing in your ear or sniffing very loudly every thirty seconds. Just when you think there will be some respite, and you have recovered from the racing heart caused by the last blast, the next wave of blorting and snorting comes cascading out of their germ-ridden orifices to wake you from your slumber.

RARITY
7 – surprisingly, the Hero is quite common. When you think that around three months of the year are covered by the winter period, and a further three to four months coincide with the hay fever season, then for over 50 per cent of your commuting year you should expect to come into contact with the Hero. Then of course there is the occasional illness gifted to us by our progeny, which must account for at least another month's worth of snot and phlegm and occasionally vomit. So all in all, two thirds of the year may be ruined.

SEASONAL VARIATIONS
There is no doubt that the Hero comes out in larger numbers during the **winter months**. As Autumn turns to winter the spluttering, retching, sniffing, throat clearing and sneezing begins. But we mustn't forget the impact of children (principally those at school) as once they get a cold, we can guarantee that everyone else will too, or summer when hay fever is all the rage. Expect a lot more sneezing and plenty of phlegm in the air from May through to September.

AVOIDANCE / REVENGE STRATEGIES
1. Wear ear defenders, face mask and goggles during the high-risk periods.

2. Take a towel to wipe yourself down.

3. Take a box of tissues with you and offer it to the Hero.

4. Get hold of some anti-bacterial spray and go on the offensive.

5. Catch an highly infectious disease, such as the bubonic plague or SARS and sit next to the Hero – let's see them drag themselves into work after contracting this one.

☐ Tick here when you have spotted the Hero

RATE THE **HERO'S** ANNOYANCE

The High-Flier

GENERAL CHARACTERISTICS

I was in Florida one Easter, sitting in a restaurant on the coast at Key Largo when a middle-aged, potbellied man walked into the restaurant. He was wearing a T-shirt with the following caption "I'm not unemployed, I'm a consultant". An insight into our age perhaps, as it seems that everyone is or wants to be as high flying as the consultant. But the true High-Flier is one who is armed with a laptop, mobile phone, earnest look and a wealth of tales about the far-flung places they have visited and the organisations they have worked for. And, of course, their British Airways Gold Card which will be sticking obtrusively from their laptop bag or briefcase. These things are only used by the High-Flier and the Social Climber. All of these attributes have an amazing capability to irritate you, not least because of the aplomb with which they carry it off. The High-Flier will place their utensils on the table before them in the same way a student does in the exam hall. They wait patiently as their laptop boots up, not knowing what to do with themselves. Do they stare at people, look out of the window, look down at their groin or stare lovingly at the screen? Most do the latter. Once fully operational they type away, patiently waiting for the incoming call from their most valued client/boss: "Hi, George, how are you?" (as if they cared). After taking their *essential* call they put their phone down and carry on typing. The keyboard skills of the High-Flier leave a lot to be desired as some love to type loudly to the point where you think they will break the keyboard (if only they would). Indeed, one colleague

of mine has managed to get through five keypads in two years! A true High-Flier if ever there was one. A friend of mine was travelling into work one morning and a guy opposite him was typing away with the usual intense look about him. Tap, tap, TAP, **TAP**, **TAP**! The noise was apparently so deafening that he was disturbing everyone in the carriage. My friend raised his head above his paper and said "Do you really have to make so much goddamn noise when you type?" The man looked surprised and said "Mind your own business, I'm busy". My friend replied "Well, why don't you be busy and noisy somewhere else?" The man got up and went to a different carriage and the remaining commuters cheered. It seems that everyone detests the noise but, as always, few are willing to take any action. But it is not just the noise they make. The High-Flier also has the tendency to brag. I was on the train home some time ago was listening to two High-Fliers inform each other of the busy overseas schedules they had and how it would be such a relief to have some time off at Christmas. In the space of about thirty minutes they had mentioned practically every country in the world and virtually every capital city. "Oh, I remember the assignment in Shanghai, it was very difficult and I had to really tune into the Chinese culture," said one. "I couldn't agree more. In fact, when I was in Nigeria I had to contend with all those beggars," said the other. The conversation was delivered with treacly sensitivity – these guys actually meant it. Unlike the Traveller, the High-Flier's name dropping is always work based but just as annoying. Both were really trying to outdo the other but obviously felt obliged to show some empathy and interest, false though it was.

ANNOYANCE RATING

7 – The High-Flier is aggravating because of the combination of aloofness, seriousness, name dropping, intellectual masturbation and the lack of keyboard skills. Surely they stop working some times, or is it all for show? I know of plenty of High-Fliers who like to appear busy, but actually deliver zip.

RARITY

8 – The High-Flier is very common, although their numbers, like the Investment Banker are falling fast with the contraction of the global economy. So in the medium term they might reduce but as everyone wants to be a High-Flier, it won't be long before their numbers recover and we will all be swamped by the army of laptop-toting businessmen.

SEASONAL VARIATIONS

High-Fliers do not change with the season. You will see them every day and on every train.

AVOIDANCE / REVENGE STRATEGIES

1. Avoid people with laptops.

2. Offer the High-Flier use of your extra thick woollen gloves to reduce the noise when they are typing.

3. Pretend to be a potential client who, on overhearing their conversation, is interested in understanding about what they can offer in supply chain management. Ask for a card and never ring them.

4. Cut up their frequent flyer card.

5. Explain to them that a recent survey placed High-Fliers beneath Porn Stars and Estate Agents as people who you can trust.

☐ Tick here when you have spotted the High-Flier

RATE THE **HIGH-FLIER'S** ANNOYANCE

The Late Starter

Many of us are poor timekeepers and we are all guilty of leaving things to the last minute. It must be human nature. But when it comes to trains it is, in my humble opinion, unforgivable. The Late Starter applies not only to the person who decides to join the train as it is about to leave the station but also to the train driver. How many times have I, and my commuting fraternity, sat on a train waiting for it to leave on time only to be disappointed; almost every day. Punctuality is a dirty word. The usual excuses apply: signal failures, leaves on the track, rain, broken down trains and so on and so on. But if that is not enough to contend with you get the commuters who feel that making a dash for a train which is just about to depart is a fantastic way to start and end the day. The Late Starter is someone who is generally disorganised and is an incredibly poor timekeeper. Everything in their life is left to the last minute and catching a train is no exception. You see them sprint out of the ticket barriers like a greyhound from a trap. They push people out of the way, stumble as they trip over dawdlers and shout "Excuse me, excuse me!" as they force their way through the massed army of commuters all trying to get on themselves. Then they have a choice. Do they push their way into an already overcrowded doorway, thereby instantly becoming a Sardine Packer, or do they continue their Olympic run to find a partially filled carriage in the hope of securing the elusive double seat? Invariably it will be the former because they just don't have the time. They

enter the carriage huffing and puffing, gasping for every breath and perspiring heavily. The Late Starter is particularly annoying on slam door trains. Because these do not have an automatic closing mechanism people run for the train even as it is beginning to move out of the station. They hang on to the doors desperately trying to get them open in order to leap onto the train. Everyone on the inside looks out and collectively thinks "What a w****r." I recently witnessed a near fist-fight between a station guard and a passenger. As the guard shouted "Stand away please! Sir, will you stand away from the door now?" the guy continued in his quest and asked "Where's this train going to?" "It doesn't matter Sir, will you stand back from the door please, the train is departing!" "Look, all I want to know if this train is going to Salisbury." "Stand away now or I will call the Police!" "No, I won't, just tell me where this bloody train is going to!" Finally, the guard manhandled the man away from the door and train slowly moved along the tracks. The argument continued on the platform with the commuter shouting at the guard "Give me your name and I'll have you sacked!" I'm sure it all ended amicably. The Late Starter is willing to risk life and limb in order to get onto their train. The Late Starter has a friend, the Late Finisher. This is the person who realises (too late of course) that they are at their stop and attempts to squeeze through the closing doors only to get stuck in the process. The best example of this was described to me by a friend. A chap leapt up after the train had stopped and everyone who wanted to get off had done so. He flung himself through the sliding doors as they closed. As he did so they either caught his case, or the G force as he whipped his arm and case through the ever-decreasing gap flung the case open and spewed its contents – which turned out to be ladies' underwear – into the train as the doors shut. He ran off somewhat embarrassed.

ANNOYANCE RATING

4 – The Late Starter is annoying, of that I have no doubt. But just how severe very much depends on your state of mind. If you are in a relaxed mood and don't have any real time pressure to get to work or home, then you can let their moronic behaviour just wash over you. However, if you have had the usual horrible day or if you have a vital meeting you must attend then the Late Starter is bound to raise your blood pressure.

RARITY

6 – As the remaining slam door trains are taken out of service, sold off to India or just scrapped, the ability of the Late Starter to delay your journey will reduce. Until then, however, there are plenty of them around. I see many every day frantically tearing along station platforms like men and women possessed. Is it worth it in the great scheme of things?

SEASONAL VARIATIONS

There are **few real seasonal changes** in the Late Starter's behaviour. You might sometimes see a few more during the **holiday season** as tourists and families not used to trains run along the platform as they realise they have got precisely fifty seconds to get them and their baggage onto the train. No hope, I'm afraid.

AVOIDANCE / REVENGE STRATEGIES

1. Never travel on slam door trains.

2. Stand right next to the door so that it appears that the carriage is full. Hopefully the Late Starter will move on to the next door.

3. If you are on a train with automatic doors, press the close button as soon as you get on.

4. Get hold of some fake sick from a joke shop and leave it in the doorway.

5. Arm yourself with a sword and musket and prepare to repel borders.

☐ Tick here when you have spotted the Late Starter

RATE THE
LATE STARTER'S
ANNOYANCE

The Lovers

GENERAL CHARACTERISTICS

To be in love is an intoxicating experience, of that there can be no doubt. I still am. But for many people love, and especially sex, takes a back seat as they get older or when other things get in the way like work, children and life in general. No one likes to discuss sex in public or indeed see any evidence of it, so when the Lovers appear this can lead to some embarrassed looks and raised eyebrows. The Lovers come in a number of forms, including:

* **The new lovers**
* **The serial daters** who have had more partners than most of us have had hot dinners
* **The clandestine lovers** who are typically both married to other people but are having an affair
* **The renewed interest lovers** who have been given a second lease of life by modern wonder drugs like Viagra.

The Lovers' behaviour can range from the odd peck on the cheek to non-stop French kissing and right through to full blown sex. And if you don't think that last ever happens, think again. According to some research carried out a few years ago on train seats they found – amongst the cat and dog hairs – three varieties of semen. So next time you sit down, take a tissue. There are plenty of stories about

the Lovers, including the following. One pair of students were discussing how they were to split up from their respective partners. The woman, a young blonde, and her hippie-looking boyfriend were discussing how her current boyfriend was a player (sleeping around) and how she wanted to ditch him. But it was more complex than that. The guy opposite was also one of her many exes. He said "When I was cheating on you, I put a heck of a lot of effort into our relationship". She said that she knew he'd been cheating on her. Yikes, what an incredibly naive girl and one who will be destined to mess up her life. As students, of course, they were highly inarticulate, not capable of stringing more than one word together that made sense without saying "you know" every thirty seconds. Then there was the loud mobile phone conversation between a gay couple who were clearly going through a rough patch. The argument concerned Valentines Day. "I can't believe it, you've done what? As far as I'm concerned you can throw the flowers in the bin." "No Michael, I am not going to forgive you, it's Valentines Day and I expect more from you than that." "Well, you go off and shag Peter then, see if care." "You're so wicked, I hate you." This exchange went on for quite some time and only finished when he reached his stop. After he got off the carriage erupted with laughter. Then there is the wonderful story that hit the media a couple of years ago concerning a couple making passionate love on a packed train. Not one person raised an objection. Most either diverted their eyes, busied themselves with some work, buried their heads in their books or did anything they could to ignore the succession of grunts and pants as the couple went at it like a steam engine. Only once they had completed their act and lit up cigarettes did the tirade of abuse follow. Not about their lovemaking, you understand, but about them smoking in a non-smoking carriage. Once again the anal retentiveness of the average commuter comes out strongly. If there was a "no sex" sign they would have been up in arms, but without it they did not have the permission to protest.

ANNOYANCE RATING

4 – this depends on how close the Lovers are to you and on your general attitudes to sex in public. Given that most Lovers tend to spend their journey either on their mobile phones whispering sweet nothings to their loved one, or seeing how far they can push their tongue down their partner's throat they don't present too much of a distraction. As I have never witnessed people having sex on a train I can't vouch for how annoying they would be. Maybe you might know?

RARITY

1 – The real, all-hands-to-the-pumps type Lovers are exceptionally rare and may even be an urban myth. I can see the appeal of joining the Mile High Club (making love with a perfect stranger in a plane, either in the toilet or in Business Class). But in a decrepit old train? Perhaps there is such a thing as the Three Foot Club.

SEASONAL VARIATIONS

Once again the onset of **Spring** and the effects of alcohol play their part. One notices a larger number of commuters snogging on the journey home during the spring and summer months than during the winter. You also witness more groin rubbing and massaging too.

AVOIDANCE / REVENGE STRATEGIES

1. Sit at a table to avoid seeing the Lovers' below the waist activities.

2. Buy some sunglasses which are mirrored on the inside.

3. Carry an illustrated edition of the Karma Sutra and offer it to the Lovers to help them adopt a position suitable for train travel. Maybe a book – the Train Sutra – should be published?

4. Film the Lovers' antics and let them know you are an amateur porn director.

5. Carry a packet of condoms and offer them to the Lovers whilst giving them a lecture on safe sex.

☐ Tick here when you have spotted the Lovers

The Make Up Artist

GENERAL CHARACTERISTICS

The Make Up Artist is one of the few Pains that is exclusively female, apart from Transvestites. But as I have never seen one, we'll assume this is a woman-only Pain. The Make Up Artist adorns herself in public, applying rouge, mascara, blusher, lip gloss and other toiletries with the contemptuous arrogance which implies that the rest of the carriage is not worthy of being her audience. The fact they can't get up a bit earlier and apply their make up before joining the train is one of the great wonders of the modern world. How the make up is applied will depend exclusively on the type of rolling stock the Make Up Artist happens to be travelling on. The newer trains, which afford table space, allow the Make Up Artist to spread compacts, lipstick, gloss and various other apparatus around the table. Some even go to the lengths of including a medium sized mirror. For those Make Up Artists that travel on rolling stock without tables the knack of applying their face paint is significantly harder. It's comical to watch as they sit in their beautifully ironed clothes holding a mirror in one hand and mascara in the other, with the utensils balanced precariously on their lap. They sway from side to side in tune with the train movements, bouncing up and down as the imperfections of the rails are played out in the carriage, all timed carefully to avoid slippage and spillage. Under these circumstances you have to admire their expertise and perseverance. Many get the timing wrong and end up with lipstick half way up their cheek.

Commuters have pointed out an amazing fact about the Make Up Artist, which you really must try to observe if you can. As they apply their make up, especially mascara and eye liner, they can't help but keep their mouth wide open. Just picture a woman swaying from side to side in the carriage, a gaping cavern of a mouth, eyes like dinner plates and head bobbing up and down as the mascara is applied. A friend of mine was recently travelling into work from Windsor. The lady opposite spent most of the journey prettying herself and for her finale she sprayed herself with a perfume that caught the back of her fellow commuters' throats. The Lady next to him discreetly held her hanky over her mouth and nose, whilst he waggled his broadsheet to waft the acrid stench away. Once again, all executed without a single complaint!

ANNOYANCE VALUE
8 – for some reason, the Make Up Artist seems to annoy other commuters and especially those women who are much better organised in the mornings. As for men, I think they find it mildly amusing to watch some old witch apply her make up in the most inconvenient of places.

RARITY
8 – with so many more women following important, city-based careers, the number of Make Up Artists has ballooned. Indeed, you should expect to see them every day. However, the Make Up Artist is very much a morning phenomenon because they need to look their best for their boss, staff and clients. Coming home is a different matter. Their faces look puffy, the jowls sag, their eyes look blackened from fatigue and their eyeliner is smudged. They go to work looking like princesses and come home looking like drag queens.

SEASONAL VARIATIONS
Although there are **no seasonal variations** in the numbers of Make Up Artists, you are likely to observe some changes in what they slap onto their pasty skin. During the autumn you should spot browns and rusts, in winter the much darker colours and especially black, spring the yellows and oranges and in summer the reds and pinks.

AVOIDANCE / REVENGE STRATEGIES
1. Sit around men. Most do not apply make up, at least not on weekdays.

2. Offer them advice on colours, saying "Oh, I don't think that really suits your complexion, it would be much better if you wore yellow".

3. Fidget, read broadsheet papers and generally move as much as possible to disrupt the application process.

4. Wear a tee-shirt with a suitable antivivisectionist caption like "Make-up kills bunnies".

5. Offer them a trowel with which to apply their make up. They can slap a lot more on than with a brush. It's faster too.

☐ Tick here when you have spotted the Make Up Artist

RATE THE
MAKE UP ARTIST'S
ANNOYANCE

The Mammoth

GENERAL CHARACTERISTICS

Be in no doubt, the world is getting fatter. Obesity is on the rise. There are now 1.1 billion people in the word who are clinically and dangerously obese. Anyone travelling across the United States will see this firsthand – fat people travelling about on their special motorised wheelchairs so that they can get to their next burger joint. This, of course, is not a solely American phenomenon as the United Kingdom, Europe and most countries around the world are experiencing similar changes in girth. In the UK there are around eight million obese people. Unfortunately this has implications for the embattled train user. The rolling stock on which we travel is designed for the more lithe and slim amongst us. This means that if you ever have the misfortune of sitting next to someone who is so large that they take up more than a single seat, you are destined to have an uncomfortable journey. Maybe the train operating companies need to do what the airlines do and charge the rotundly-challenged double but I don't think they have cottoned on to this just yet. It might be a fantastic way to increase profits. The makers of new rolling stock also seem to be behind the curve when it comes to population trends. They seem to be making seats smaller, not larger, which does not bode well. The only consolation is that you have arm rests. The new rolling stock with airline seats means that the Mammoth has to literally prise himself into and out of the space, which is a delicate operation and one you certainly don't want to be a party to. And, if you do have the misfortune of sitting

on the inside seat (next to the window) remember to start the process of getting off at least two stops before your station, as otherwise you might not be able to leave at all. I recall one morning travelling to work when the all too familiar "I'm sorry to announce…" mantra bellowed out from the public address system. The train that I was due to join was to terminate because it was defective. I, along with at least two hundred other people, legged it for the slow train that was due to depart from Platform 1. The train was nearly full, and I managed to get a seat in a carriage that had space for four normally-sized people. There were two spaces left. One next to myself and one by a slight gentleman who was sitting opposite. The defective train pulled into the station and everyone from that train piled onto the one I was sitting on. Within a couple of minutes I had a woman sitting next to me. With one smallish space left, who should appear but one of the largest men I had ever seen. Huffing and puffing he forced his way through the narrow doorway and plonked himself in the tiny space across from me. The poor chap opposite looked as though his very existence was about to be squashed out of him. He let out an almighty squeal as his upper thigh was crushed under the Mammoth's weight. No apology though, and I had to bite my tongue to stop from laughing. The little guy then spent the rest of the journey perched on the edge of his seat (there was no room left apart from an envelope sized portion, which even he couldn't fit into) desperately trying to avoid any bodily contact. Other stories include how one summer a Mammoth's fat literally rolled over the arm rest to invade the space of the woman next to him. Unfortunately, it being summer, he was sweating profusely and by the end of the commute the blouse of the poor lady concerned was soaking wet.

ANNOYANCE RATING

8 – the annoyance very much depends on whether you like a skip-load of flesh rammed against your body for fifty minutes. If you like it then the irritation is limited. But, if you are like most of the commuting population who find it repulsive, then the annoyance rating rises rapidly.

RARITY

5 – at the current time, at least, we don't see too many Mammoths on the trains. However, with the increased number of obese people, I am sure we will. Indeed in the UK at least, it is expected that within ten to fifteen years over seventy-five per cent of people will be overweight. Perhaps if this book is ever revised, it might be the thin person who is the Pain, because everyone else will be gargantuan.

SEASONAL VARIATIONS

Summer often sees an increased proportion of overseas Mammoths, particularly Americans and Germans. What is so disgusting is their preference for ill-fitting T-shirts and shorts which leave nothing to the imagination. One benefit during winter is that the Mammoth can be used as a great source of heat. So next time you're feeling cold in a freezing carriage, seek out a Mammoth to sit next to. You don't have to be too close to benefit from the radiation from their immense body.

AVOIDANCE / REVENGE STRATEGIES

1. Always sit next to a very thin person.

2. Place as many bags and items of clothing next to your seat as you can and pretend to be asleep – if the Mammoth is sensitive they won't disturb you. And, remember, you mustn't respond to their prods or gentle words designed to wake you.

3. Carry a "How to Lose 200lbs in 30 Days" diet book.

4. Stick a pin in them to see if they will burst.

5. Buy one of those rubber sumo suits and wear it to work. No one will want to sit next to you, not even the Mammoth.

☐ Tick here when you have spotted the Mammoth

RATE THE
MAMMOTH'S
ANNOYANCE

The Mobile Phoner

GENERAL CHARACTERISTICS

Research has revealed that nearly half of young adults have very strong feelings about their mobile phones, describing their loss as similar to bereavement. This same research indicated that we are all increasingly emotionally dependent on them for our identity and feelings of self worth. And nearly half of us rely on the phone to lift our mood. Now that's sad. The Mobile Phoner is perhaps the king of the Pains. You hear them every morning and every evening. "Hello, where are you?" "I'm on the train." "I'm on the five fifteen, which should be in around six o'clock." As if they didn't know. Hubby has been on the same train for the past fifteen years. "Hello, it's me. I thought you would like to know that the train is running ten minutes late and you might want to ring up National Rail Enquiries to find out when it will arrive. I think the number is on your Palm under trains." It would take a moron not to realise that their other half, partner, or friend, who regularly commutes, was on the train. Maybe the wives insist on their husbands ringing them so that they can pack off their lovers before he walks through the front door. But it's not just the people ringing in, it's the train travellers that are ringing home. I really can't fathom it out. The Mobile Phoner will use their phone to ring up anyone they can just to use it. It seems to burn a hole in their pocket and they seem incapable of leaving it switched off. Just how many times have I listened to some arse ringing everyone they possibly can just to go over the trivial events of their day again, again and again. By the end of the

journey, I could write their biography – short and dull though it would be. What is odd is that everyone around the Mobile Phoner seems put out and yet, within a couple of minutes, they are doing precisely the same thing. It's a form of Mexican wave, once one person has finished their inane call, the next one pipes up. As might be expected there are many stories to tell about the Mobile Phoner. One acquaintance recalled the following. Commuting home one evening, she was sitting opposite a man who was engaged in a call with his wife. "Hello. I'm sorry, but I am late… I know it's the third time this week… It's work… I'm so sorry… I know I promised… I'll be home early tomorrow." Frustrated by this, the woman piped up in a very loud voice "Hurry up, darling, we've got to go. I can't wait for you forever." It was clear from the bright scarlet that the man turned that his wife had heard. Naturally he shut up and was suitably silent all the way home. We all tolerate the Mobile Phoner, but rarely do we act. The only exception to this is the new quiet carriage phenomenon, which is now giving people the permission to take direct action. It is great to observe as they march up and down the carriage acting as the quiet carriage police. Apart from shouting down the phone, Mobile Phoners also spend hours tinkering with the ring tones. Everything from film and television theme tunes to classical music. The question is – why do they have to be set on such loud settings, are the users deaf? Probably the best story I have ever heard was this. A man who was obviously being irritated by the Mobile Phoner next to him, interrupted to ask about his phone. "What phone have you got?" he asked. "It's a Vodafone," came the reply. "What features does it have?" he continued. "Well, it has text messaging, games and I can divert my office number to it…" This line of questioning went on for quite a few minutes, as the man enquired about every aspect of the Mobile Phoner's phone. He finished his enquiry by asking if it was insured. "Oh, of course," the Mobile Phoner responded. The man then picked up the phone, threw it out of the open window and walked off.

ANNOYANCE RATING
10 – the Mobile Phoner is getting to be one of the biggest Pains around. It's the continuous stream of verbal diarrhoea spewed out in infinite detail that really gets on your nerves. Surely it can wait until they get home. Or maybe they are so used to speaking with a lump of plastic stuck to the side of their head that this is the only way they can communicate. It won't be long before they will be sending videos of themselves which will make it even worse. The Mobile Phoner is universally detested and yet we are all guilty of falling into the trap of being what I consider the most common Pain you will meet.

RARITY
10 – The Mobile Phoner is very common and their presence continues to grow as the mobile becomes the fashion accessory to be seen with. I long for a time when the smoking carriage is replaced with the mobile phone carriage, where all the Mobile Phoners can, shout, make their calls, play games, take videos and check out the latest ring tones isolated from the rest of the train.

SEASONAL VARIATIONS
None, the Mobile Phoner likes to fry their brains every day of the year.

AVOIDANCE / REVENGE STRATEGIES
1. Sit in a quiet carriage, a long shot, but it might just work.

2. Hold you ears and scream loudly every time anyone near you uses their phone.

3. Buy a huge inflatable mobile phone and shout "Hello..Hello, I'm on the train!" into it.

4. Buy a jamming device and switch it on as soon as you get on.

5. Seize their phone, stamp on it and tell them you are conducting some research into the resilience of phone equipment.

☐ Tick here when you have spotted the Mobile Phoner

RATE THE
MOBILE PHONER'S
ANNOYANCE

The New Worker

GENERAL CHARACTERISTICS

The New Worker is full of energy, enthusiasm and excitement at the prospect of a power-packed career spanning thirty-odd years. It's great to observe, if only because you know that within two to three years they will be as disillusioned as the rest of us and hoping to downshift their life. But we should not put them down, there is nothing wrong with a bit of enthusiasm. The New Worker talks about their salary (not always that large), how fascinating their work is and how wonderful everyone is to them. "It's a great place to work. Everyone wants to talk to you and the induction course was fantastic." Coming home one evening I overheard the conversation of a New Worker. He was not earning that much, but was waxing lyrical to a friend on the other end of the phone who was in a similar position. "It's amazing what you can do with a slo cooker and it doesn't cost much at all." "I know you don't have much money left at the end of the month, but you make it stretch if you want to." "I normally visit the market to see what bargains I can pick up." "I also don't go to the launderette that often and I normally wear my underwear for two to three days. This saves me lots of cash." Then there are the new city workers. They have managed to secure a "wonderful" job earning vastly more than the average income. They love to ring up all their newly-graduated friends and say such things as "Yeah, I'm on thirty-five grand and I'm so loaded I can't believe it." "It's great, and I get this Audi TT which is a real babe magnet." "I reckon I'm in line for a huge bonus as I am told I'm

doing so well!" A colleague of mine told me about the following conversation he heard between two New Workers. "I love the company I work for, it's so wacky!" said one. "What do you mean?" asked his inquisitive companion. "Well, the only way I can get to my office is down a kiddies slide! It takes me right to my desk." "Wow, how cool is that," came the reply. Needless to say this guy was working in the New Economy so I expect he is unemployed now, or perhaps a playground attendant. You can normally spot the New Worker by their cheap shiny suit, patent leather shoes, un-scuffed briefcase and unbridled keenness. Their eyes do not have the classic signs of a long working life – drawn, vacant and with very large bags. I witnessed another conversation between two New Workers from different companies who were exchanging notes. The young lady who was, for a reason only known to herself, using a book stand (the ones used for cookery) to hold her tatty paperback, engaged a scruffy-looking young man in his twenties about work. His voice was particularly annoying because everything he said was broken up in staccato fashion and delivered almost at the top of his voice. The topics ranged from whether they were allowed to dress down, what facilities they had such as kitchens and drinks machines, why they lived outside London and commuted in, how they got to work during rail strikes, drinking and getting drunk (of course), and train timetables. If the girl was trying to chat the chap up she was making an appalling job of it. Mind you, so was he. No chance that they would become the Lovers, then.

ANNOYANCE RATING
7 – The New Worker loves work and for that they should be praised; someone has to pay for our pensions after all. Unfortunately they are too treacly and fanatical about what they do for the more seasoned commuter to cope with. If they turned it down a bit they wouldn't be quite so annoying.

RARITY
4 – the number of New Workers is steadily declining as we all get older. Over the next two decades or so, the number of young people entering the workplace will steadily decline. They will be replaced by the Miserable Old Git (hmmm, is that me?) who, because of successive raids on pensions by central government and reductions in fringe benefits offered by employers, will be working well into their eighties. By this time the New Worker will be extinct.

SEASONAL VARIATIONS
The **Autumn** is the perfect time to spot the New Worker. Fresh from university and embarking on their first real job they sit on the train in a high state of alertness. They spend time sorting through their empty briefcases (yet to be weighed down with important papers). They caress their laptops as though these were their lovers and talk fondly of their company cars. Wait until winter, when it's raining.

AVOIDANCE / REVENGE STRATEGIES
1. Sit next to a pensioner.

2. Wear some steel toe-capped boots and scuff their new briefcase.

3. Stare at them until they shut up.

4. Strategically place articles about how much money they need to save for a comfortable retirement.

5. Belch loudly into their ear.

☐ Tick here when you have spotted the New Worker

RATE THE
NEW WORKER'S
ANNOYANCE

The Night Clubbers

GENERAL CHARACTERISTICS

The Night Clubbers are another Group Pain. As the name suggests the Night Clubbers are a nocturnal Pain that comes out only on Friday, Saturday and Sunday evenings. The Night Clubbers usually comprise adolescents, the twenty-somethings and more desperate people in their thirties and forties looking for a good time. In the case of the forty-year-plus age bracket a good time often means they are desperate for sex. Those over fifty go to tea dances so you should spot few of them. The Night Clubbers head to their destination in the early evening, dressed to the nines - gold chains, medallions and as much jewellery as they can muster. They reek of perfume and aftershave. The women are in short skirts, high heels and skimpy blouses while the gents in the party wear jeans or cheap chinos with short-sleeved shirts hanging over their paunches. These days you can also spot the Night Clubbers dressed in school uniform travelling to the *School Reunion* events that are all the rage. Irrespective of dress, all Night Clubbers are hoping to pull the opposite sex, get bladdered and have a thoroughly *wicked* time. The problem for the normal train traveller is that they have to put up with their behaviour as they head out to their destination and, if particularly unfortunate, on the way home. On the way out you may experience rowdiness, shouting, abuse and general disruption. The return leg entails watching them act out some of the other Pains including the Lovers, the Drunk and the Vomiter. I experienced the Night Clubbers regularly for three years as a student. I

would travel into London to pick up a bus to take me up north late on a Sunday evening. At Harlow a group of perhaps thirty-five Night Clubbers would join the train and run amok. As it was the last train into London most were very much the worse for wear. In those days they were wearing shell suits, baseball caps and vast amounts of Bling, Bling jewellery. They shouted, intimidated other passengers and threw their empty cans of larger around the carriage. Occasionally fights broke out between the youths and before long police were patrolling the train. It was not a pleasant experience. But you should expect extremes where it comes to the Night Clubbers. According to one of my colleagues at work, bumping into the Night Clubbers in the morning is a far worse affair. After a recent stag do some of his acquaintances stayed out all night and took the 9 a.m. train back to Newcastle from Edinburgh. They were in the same alcohol/cigarette/sick-ridden clothes as the previous evening, still hideously drunk and behaving in full party mode. Any attempts at reasoning with them invited an unpleasant response. Eventually the guard intervened and had them expelled from the train.

ANNOYANCE RATING

9 – The Night Clubbers are one of the most annoying Pains because they are the most threatening and disturbing.

RARITY

7 – Nearly every major town has some kind of nightclub so you should expect to see plenty of the Night Clubbers most weekends as this is when all the slappers and lowlifes come out to play.

SEASONAL VARIATIONS

As with anything that involves revellers, the **chief festivals** will bring out more Night Clubbers than usual. The usual suspects such as **Christmas and New Year** apply but also watch out for the rock festivals as this will bring out some of the rarer forms of the Night Clubbers, including the aging hippie and the chilled out executive trying to re-establish their lost youth. And don't forget stag nights and hen parties.

AVOIDANCE / REVENGE STRATEGIES

1. Avoid travelling on a Friday, Saturday or Sunday evening.

2. Curl up into a small ball and look non-threatening.

3. Carry a baseball bat for self-defence.

4. Pull the emergency cable. No one will suspect you and will automatically blame one of the Night Clubbers.

5. Wear a police uniform and march up and down the train fondling your truncheon.

☐ Tick here when you have spotted the Night Clubber

RATE THE
NIGHT CLUBBER'S
ANNOYANCE

The Nose Picker

GENERAL CHARACTERISTICS

There is nothing more satisfying than hooking out a particularly stubborn piece of snot. As it dislodges itself from the inside of your nose and flies through the air it looks as graceful as a swan. With the wetter variety, there is the satisfaction of rolling it up into a ball and flicking it at some unsuspecting victim. Then there is the wealth of opportunities to spread it onto the chair, the armrest, the wall, in fact anywhere but a tissue. Like retirement, picking your nose is a great leveller. It doesn't matter if you are a general, top flight lawyer, priest or general labourer, picking your nose exposes your basic animal behaviour. The Nose Picker will adopt a variety of strategies to hide their activities. Some will use the safety of the newspaper to take the odd dip or two and if no one is observing them they will smear snot onto the pages. I pity the poor person who might pick the paper up to read later, but then they probably deserve it having not purchased their own. Others will use the sleeve of their jacket to help drag out the long-persistent product of their over-active nasal lining. Some will look fondly at the bogey, roll it in their hands like a good cigar and the pick it apart before daubing it on the edge of their chair. A woman commuter told me about one guy who after having rolled up the blob of snot, placed it on the end of his tongue and proceeded to chew it quite deliberately before spitting it out into his empty bag of crisps. She was almost sick. I think I would have been. If you look carefully you can see the product of the Nose Picker's actions all round the carriage. Telltale

discoloration and yellow crustaceans adorn the windows, walls and underside of the tables and, of course, there are the snail-like trails on the seats. For those Pain Spotters who are up for a bigger challenge, see if you can spot the following varieties of Nose Picker:

* **The Potholer –** digging deep is their trade mark
* **The Wine Connoisseur –** the person who savours the snot before depositing it
* **The Wet 'n' Wild –** no amount of tissues will help this poor fellow
* **The Tug 'o' War –** long sinews of snot that seem impossible to extract
* **The Fruit Picker –** so used to picking ten thousand gooseberries every day that they think they're back on the farm.
* **The Crustacean –** no snot, just scabs come from this Nose Picker.

ANNOYANCE RATING

5 – There are a number of factors that will impact how annoyed you might be with the Nose Picker, including:

* The look and feel of the snot as it comes out from their nose – is it crusty or is it long green and stringy?
* Whether they pick their nose openly or hide behind a newspaper
* Where they flick it
* Whether they wipe it in their hair
* Whether they eat it.

RARITY

7 – I see quite a lot of the Nose Picker on the trains and I certainly see the product of their actions smeared over the walls, windows and seats.

SEASONAL VARIATIONS

You are bound to see many more Nose Pickers during the **winter months** when more of us have colds. Unfortunately a lot of people run out of tissues and end up having long viscous strips hanging from the end of their nose (see the Hero). Despite the greater concentration of Nose Pickers during cold weather, you should expect to spot them every day.

AVOIDANCE / REVENGE STRATEGIES

1. Watch out for people with green fingers but don't be fooled into thinking it's because they are a gardener.

2. Always check the seats for bogies. In particular look at the edges and fronts as these are prime locations for the Nose Picker's deposits.

3. Carry a box of tissues (as you would for the Hero) and offer one to the Nose Picker.

4. Outdo the Nose Picker by buying a tub of theatrical slime and inserting it up your nose, then proceed to pull it out slowly with both hands.

5. Just as they stick their finger up their nose for the tenth time, nudge them violently so that they miss their nose and hit their eye.

☐ Tick here when you have spotted the Nose Picker

RATE THE
NOSE PICKER'S
ANNOYANCE

The Nutter

GENERAL CHARACTERISTICS

The Nutter is a class of Pain that displays some very strange behaviours indeed and does not follow the conventions of the other Pains. They also provide the greatest form of amusement (or annoyance) for the commuter. They come in all shapes and sizes, and from all walks of life. Stories of the Nutter are legion amongst the commuting population. Here are some of the many:

* **The woman who would bring her dog onto the train** every morning and feed it dog food from her hand. Once the dog had finished the woman would smear the remaining food and dog saliva on the seat next to her. Apparently you could see some commuters visibly retch whilst she did so.

* **The phantom raspberry blower.** A commuter was travelling on a packed train one afternoon. There was little space and the air was thin. Then he heard a gentle rasp. People looked at each other with the "It wasn't me" look about them as they thought it was another case of the Phantom Farter. A couple of minutes later there was another rasp, this time a little louder. Eyes turned upward and again everybody did everything to avoid eye contact. This went on for some time, until a sharp-eyed commuter spotted the source of the noise. An old woman was blowing raspberries behind her paper. Every minute or so she would purse her lips and blow.

- I am sure you've seen them, **the devout nutter who takes out a bible** on the morning commute and begins to recite selected passages from Corinthians or Revelations. When they do, they look up in the hope of spotting someone whom they can have a deeply existential discussion with, if only to inform them that they are going to Hell. In a secular society such behaviour is indeed strange. Surely people go to church for that?

- A colleague was travelling on a train once when **a man stood up and announced that he had once appeared on the quiz show Mastermind** and that he was the only contestant to get every question wrong. He then went on to explain what a traumatic effect this had had on his life and that he was as good as ruined. No one gave a tinker's cuss.

- A rare one, this. **Apparently there was this man who would urinate on the seat** opposite and then sit there with a huge grin on his face as his unsuspecting victim sat down. I gather he was eventually caught and locked away.

- **There is a Nutter who habitually travels around North London. He is a black guy in his mid thirties with a great sense of irony.** He wears a Confederate flag around his waist, smokes spliffs on the tube, and philosophises about life to anyone who'll listen (as well as those who don't). One of his greatest quotes, picked out from a twenty-minute incomprehensible monologue was as follows: "Swearing, what's wrong with swearing? Show me a f***ing deaf man that doesn't want to hear a swear word."

ANNOYANCE RATING

4 – this very much depends on the type of Nutter you come across. In general most Nutters are mildly entertaining because their actions and utterances are so bizarre that you can't help but laugh to yourself. It's also very funny watching other people react as they realise they have screwed up and sat next to a nutcase.

RARITY

3 – although quite rare, as more of us succumb to the mental degradation of old age, the stress of difficult jobs and the effects of the American psychoanalyst culture, we should expect to see more people unafraid of getting in touch with their feelings in public.

SEASONAL VARIATIONS

You tend to find more Nutters during the **party season**. I guess this is because of the effects of alcohol and drugs on the physiology of the brain. They say alcohol loosens the tongue. It clearly loosens brain cells too.

AVOIDANCE / REVENGE STRATEGIES

1. Walk.

2. Wear dark glasses, carry a white stick and pretend to be blind.

3. Pose as a psychoanalyst and ask them to make an appointment with your secretary.

4. Whip out your camera, take the Nutter's photo and inform them that you are holding a freak show at the Royal Academy next month and ask them if they would be the star attraction.

5. Sway uncontrollably and foam at the mouth. If you can't beat them, join them. You never know, someone might give you some of their loose change.

☐ Tick here when you have spotted the Nutter

RATE THE **NUTTER'S** ANNOYANCE

The Over Your Shoulder

GENERAL CHARACTERISTICS

Travelling by train provides an ideal opportunity to be nosy. Not only is it ideal for a student of human behaviour (such as myself) but it also allows those with a long beak to find out what other people are up to. Plenty of business secrets are divulged during the course of a conversation, or in important documents that really ought to be kept private. The old war adage "Careless talk costs lives" is as applicable today as ever. Who needs industrial espionage when some careless fool is bragging about their latest deal? The Over Your Shoulder is inherently curious but, unlike the Engager (whose modus operandi is to talk to those around them to glean as much as possible), the Over Your Shoulder practices his art silently. The telltale sign of an Over Your Shoulder is someone who travels to work without anything to read, often with no baggage other than a small briefcase containing a manky sandwich. They blatantly read your paper, watch as you type on your laptop, or look over what you happen to be reading or writing whilst hunched over the table. I enjoyed writing this book when in the presence of the Over Your Shoulder. They looked suitably taken aback when they found out what I was writing about – them. They are unable to help themselves, making mental notes and judgements about you and what you do. "Oh I bet he is important, maybe he works for the intelligence service," or "Hmm, I can't see what that person sees in working for a charity". I guess to some degree we all suffer from this condition as I sometimes catch myself reading a teasing headline or

looking out of the corner of my eye to admire the wonderful things people are doing with PowerPoint and wondering who they might work for. Some commuters casually position themselves to watch what I am doing. When this happens, I twist around so they can't see my laptop. As they move back I reposition myself. After a few minutes this mating dance repeats itself, and must look strangely comical. A lady commuter told me of one journey where an Over Your Shoulder persisted on leaning over and reading what she was typing on her computer. He would tut loudly and make disapproving sounds as if he were her English teacher. She would shoot the man a foul look and get back to her work. Until after fifteen minutes of this when she rounded on the chap and said "why don't you go and pester someone else?!" He turned away suitably humbled, but within a few seconds the recidivist was up to his old tricks. By now furious, she shut down her computer and barged past to move to another seat. On the way she succeeded in jolting the man's coffee over his trousers, producing a satisfying yelp of pain. The travelling public includes those who so yearn for attention that they present open invitations to the Over Your Shoulder. They carefully place key documents, with their important-sounding title, so that you can't help but read them. This is a subtle form of the Social Climber.

ANNOYANCE RATING
8 – I find the Over Your Shoulder very disconcerting because of the way they invade your personal space. Why can't they find something to entertain themselves for half an hour? It's worse than dealing with a child.

RARITY
9 – the Over Your Shoulder is very common and you can see most people at it during the course of the morning commute, when they like to read your paper, and the evening commute when they like to do it again but this time with your evening tabloid. Many will deliberately hold back on arriving at the station in order to steal your rag.

SEASONAL VARIATIONS
There are no real seasonal variations because people are nosy **all year round**. However, it is feasible that the Over Your Shoulder could transform into the Pervert or Starer especially when there are scantily clad women about.

AVOIDANCE / REVENGE STRATEGIES
1. Go to sleep when travelling by train, in this way you can avoid the Over Your Shoulder entirely.

2. Type "Are you enjoying reading this, you nosy bastard?" on your computer as you catch them slyly looking at your work.

3. Shake your paper so that they can't read it, or place a couple of Post-It notes on your paper that says "Why don't you buy your own bloody paper, tightwad?"

4. Make a curtain wall out of some old cardboard boxes and carefully place it around you to shield you from prying eyes.

5. Create a mock newspaper article with the headline "Nosy parker killed on train whilst attempting to read another person's paper." And leave it lying on the table or seat next to you.

☐ Tick here when you have spotted the Over Your Shoulder

*RATE THE **OVER YOUR SHOULDER'S** ANNOYANCE*

The Pervert

GENERAL CHARACTERISTICS

We all want to avoid the Pervert. Perverts are predominantly men who take pleasure in offending women. Some are quite passive, restricting their actions to eying women up and down (see The Starer). Others can be more active by getting closer to well-dressed or scantily-clad ladies. Others still just like to behave in a sexually offensive way. I won't labour this too much, but just provide a couple of examples. A friend of mine was travelling home quite late one evening along with his girlfriend and another woman from their office. The journey had passed without incident. As they were getting off the girlfriend turned to their female companion and said "Did you see that man?" "Yes, I did," answered her friend. "It was disgusting!" My friend asked what they were talking about. Throughout the journey, the girls had noticed a man in his twenties who was staring at them smiling. His smile widened as the journey lengthened. Only then did they spot his manhood hanging outside of his expensive pinstriped suit. Not hanging for long though, as within a short space of time, it was standing to attention and he was busy working himself into a lather. Thankfully they did not see his arrival, as they were getting off the train. When my friend asked the ladies why they had not said anything they replied "Well, we didn't want to make a fuss". As always we commuters seem to put up with anything. The guy could be classified as a single Lover or perhaps an extreme version of the Flamboyant Groin. Whatever he was his conduct was not appropriate for the commute home. It's odd,

but this type of behaviour seems to be more common than you think, as other commuters have mentioned similar events. This reminds me of a train journey up to Newcastle. It was a long trip, approximately three hours. The man opposite appeared to be exceptionally engrossed in the paper he was reading. I can't recall what it was, but it surprised me at the time how something that looked so boring could provide so much entertainment for so long. His eyes were like bowls as they flitted from left to right and he would occasionally lick his lips. A while later, he popped to the toilet. As he was taking rather a long time, I took the opportunity to look at his paper. What should I find? Only a hardcore pornographic magazine. Now I could understand why he was so immersed in his paper and why he was taking so long in the loo. He certainly looked hot under the collar when he returned. When I went to the toilet, I went to the one at the other end of the carriage. A friend of mine also mentioned the Frotteur (frottage is the sexual pleasure derived from rubbing up against the clothing of another person). On a delayed train one strike ridden summer my friend was crushed into a space at the end of a full carriage. An attractive, nicely-spoken girl in a summer frock standing next to him said apologetically "may I rub up against you, it's so crowded?" It was over ninety degrees and he was so limp and puzzled about whether the double entendre was unintentional, or whether she was sexually frustrated and it was a pass, that all he could say was "don't worry, we're all in the same boat". He is sure that the young lady was not a regular commuter, had never experienced being squashed together, and been brought up to be polite and was merely asking for an apology in advance. But he has had fantasies ever since.

ANNOYANCE RATING

10 – I'm afraid the Pervert ranks very high on the annoyance scale, if only because of their gross behaviour.

RARITY

1 – In all my discussions with commuters I have only come across a few stories that involve the Pervert, so on that basis I think we can safely say they are very rare and hopefully will remain so.

SEASONAL VARIATIONS

Summer time is likely to bring out the mild form of the Pervert. These are the people who can't help themselves when they see attractive women on the train dressed in low-cut blouses and short skirts. Some will watch each and every one of them, whilst others will dream of finding a packed train so that they can rub up against them. Luckily our climate is not hot all year round so after the summer the Pervert is suitably subdued.

AVOIDANCE / REVENGE STRATEGIES

1. Always dress like a tramp so that you won't be considered attractive.

2. Travel with a hunk who can beat up the Pervert if you spot them.

3. Carry a dart with you and throw it at the groin of the Pervert if they get out of hand.

4. Make some comment about how the Pervert's manhood looks, like "I've seen a bigger penis on a mouse!" Or perhaps call them the Chipolata Kid.

5. Pull the emergency cord and have the Pervert thrown off the train.

☐ Tick here when you have spotted the Pervert

RATE THE
PERVERT'S
ANNOYANCE

The Phantom Farter

GENERAL CHARACTERISTICS

*O*ne of the unfortunate side effects of being human is our involuntary production of malodorous gas. We do however have almost full control over how we evacuate it from our backsides. Just picture yourself. You are sitting in a packed carriage and a storm is welling up in your bowels. Although it was a great idea to have that extra hot curry the night before, it doesn't seem such a good idea now. What do you do? Will you let off an almighty parp and suffer the embarrassment as those around you point, stare and most probably pass out? Do you raise one cheek off the seat to allow the gas to escape in a steady stream? Or do you clench your buttocks and release the pungent air slowly, hoping that no one will notice that it was you and that the seat will absorb most of the warm emission? There is always the real and present danger of a silent delivery but a violent smell. Say hello to the Phantom Farter. We are all Phantom Farters and anyone who says they are not is probably lying. People react predictably when someone drops one. They display a combination of disdain and virtue. Disdain at whoever could have carried out such an appalling act in such a public place and virtue to demonstrate that it was not them. You can spot people's halos from the other end of the carriage. As the stench drifts through the carriage the reaction is like a Mexican wave. Faces crumple as the stink reaches the nose followed rapidly by the "it wasn't me" look protesting their innocence. To emphasis their purity, they look towards the person next to them or the one opposite and shoot them a

disgusted look. It is rare that the source of the pong is ever revealed so everyone starts to make assumptions about who may have perpetrated the terrible deed. They will often select the unkempt student, the prim, tight-mouthed lady or the minging old man. The biggest problem is when you are sitting next to a person who is unable to control their bowels. Passing wind once is bad enough but emitting a continuous stream of foul smelling odours all the way to work just isn't British. Every few minutes a waft from the inside of their underwear will pass across your nose. Fellow passengers will use their papers and books to disperse the gas to both escape the stench and demonstrate their blamelessness. You occasionally witness more outrageous behaviour when a group of students or youngish men travel together. Usually the worse for wear they will set fire to their farts with a lighter. Oh, what fun. Sometimes they squeal in pain as the flames travel through their underwear and into their anal canal, which is much more amusing. For the more expert or proctologists amongst us, it is possible to assess what the Phantom Farter has consumed, was it:

- **A particularly hot curry**
- **A dodgy kebab**
- **Thirty pints of real ale**
- **An enormous bowl of vegetables** (those who just eat vegetables produce some of the most intense smelling guffs around).

ANNOYANCE RATING

4 – Assuming the Phantom Farter only passes wind once, their annoyance is short lived. This might increase if they repeatedly evacuate parcels of putrid gas into the carriage, or if the smell is particularly disgusting. Fortunately the gas will dissipate quite quickly, especially if the carriage has widows.

RARITY

6 – I have suffered the consequences of the Phantom Farter often enough to believe they are quite common. You tend to find more amongst the vegetarians because of all the foliage they eat. After all, have you ever smelt a compost heap?

SEASONAL VARIATIONS

Strangely the party season seems to bring out more Phantom Farters than normal. Let me explain. The party-goer's bowels will be firing on all cylinders because of the catalytic combination of finger food and booze. And because there is a delayed effect you are more likely to meet them the following morning. Thank heavens that most people party of a Friday or Saturday night.

AVOIDANCE / REVENGE STRATEGIES

1. Avoid people with puckered lips – an early warning sign of the Phantom Farter.

2. Carry a handkerchief laced with lavender and wear it around your neck.

3. As soon as you smell the offensive odour stand up, point to its source and shout "Why don't you visit a doctor?"

4. Offer the Phantom Farter a cork to plug up their bottom.

5. Pose as a proctologist and start quizzing them about their diet and how it affects their bowel movements.

☐ Tick here when you have spotted the Phantom Farter

RATE THE
PHANTOM FARTER'S
ANNOYANCE

The Reservist

With so much overcrowding it is often a great idea to reserve your seat. This is fine until you realise:

- **The train company has not physically reserved it**
- **You find someone else sitting in it**
- **It is in a terrible mess and can't be used.**

Welcome to the Reservist. The Reservist is someone who will fight for their God-given right to sit on the seat that *they* reserved. On a long distance rail journey reserving seats is the norm and rarely presents difficulties. But when it comes to travelling during peak hours a number of rules seem to apply. Firstly, though I have never checked, it seems almost impossible to reserve a seat during the morning rush. Secondly, although you can, you would be very unwise to reserve a seat during the evening commute. And, thirdly, it is not generally a good idea to contest a Reservist's seat. As with a number of the Pains, the Reservist is someone who is not a regular train traveller and will therefore be unfamiliar with the rules of engagement. They may be old, a family or even an overseas visitor. Whatever they are, they feel duty bound to sit in their allotted seat. A colleague was travelling on an long-distance train recently. The carriage was completely empty.

As it was pulling out from one of its planned stops a middle-aged man entered the carriage, carefully checking his ticket and the seat numbers. His reserved seat happened to be directly opposite my colleague's, and he sat in it despite the other fifty or so empty ones in the same compartment. My colleague, in a state of incredulity, refused to move. The rest of the journey was spent battling for table space and leg room. A dark side of Reservist behaviour can often manifest itself on the way home. One particular evening I was sitting in the usual overcrowded train when a group of Reservists got on. They marched up to their seats only to find people sitting in them. "Excuse me," one of them said, "you're sitting in our seats." "I don't think so," came the reply. "Look," demanded the Reservist, and showed the cuckoo his ticket. The seat number coincided with the seat in question. "You look," said the chap in the seat. "This seat was not reserved. There was no ticket indicating that it was, so I am staying put. Why don't you find somewhere else to sit?" Naturally, there were no other seats and some commuters were already standing. "This is my seat," said the Reservist "and you can bloody well get out of it!" The argument became increasingly heated. Eventually the Reservist wandered off, red in the face, to return a few minutes later with the guard. The man who was occupying the seat remained steadfast. Physical tussles eventually prised him from his position. The Reservist will go to any length to claim what is rightfully theirs. In fact they are also known as the Terminator because they absolutely will not stop at anything, ever, until they have got their seat.

ANNOYANCE RATING

2 – the Reservist scores low on the annoyance rating, as unless you happen to be sitting in their seat they are likely to only distract you. In fact they can provide you with some amusing diversions on the way home. The arguments have a wonderful pantomime air about them: "Oh yes you do…Oh no you don't". However, be warned. If you are sitting in a Reservist's seat you will be hunted down mercilessly and no excuse whatsoever will be accepted. Even if you have no arms or legs you will be removed from your seat. In this instance the annoyance rating is likely to go off the scale. Of course the reverse of the reservist is the cuckoo. Just who is the Pain here?

RARITY

6 – The Reservist is not that rare really and tends to be more common on long-distance routes. Commuter trains only suffer from the Reservist's presence in the evenings.

SEASONAL VARIATIONS

There is no doubt that the **Summer** brings out more Reservists. Once again it is the usual suspects you bump into, including the Traveller and the Family.

AVOIDANCE / REVENGE STRATEGIES

1. Sit in an unreserved seat.

2. Always be prepared to eat humble pie, apologise and accept that you have been found out.

3. If you find a reserved ticket on your seat screw it up and pretend you never saw it. It might just work.

4. Pretend to be asleep, drunk or drugged up. No one in their right mind would want to disturb you.

5. Open a packet of razor blades and start playing with them whilst at the same time laughing like a mad scientist and looking round the carriage nervously.

☐ Tick here when you have spotted the Reservist

RATE THE
RESERVIST'S
ANNOYANCE

The Ritualist

When you've been commuting for a number of years your behaviours become entrenched. As we know, we are creatures of habit, standing in the same place and sitting at the same table each morning and evening. This process of going to work and coming home can become an obsessive–compulsive disorder. Think about it. When you can't get your usual train, or fail to sit in the same place you did for the last year, how do you feel? Sweat may run from your brow, or your heart miss a beat or two. You become flustered and agitated, perhaps even depressed. Such worrying signs might suggest it is time to break your routine with a long holiday from commuting, or seek advice of a psychotherapist. Here are a few examples of the Ritualist:

- **One chap travels on the same carriage as myself.** Irrespective of the weather he is parcelled up in an overcoat, thick scarf and flat cap. As he sits down he takes an inflatable neck brace from an overcoat pocket, blows it up, places it behind his neck and tilts his cap over his eyes. He spends the rest of the trip chortling to himself. What about, no one has ever fathomed out. Perhaps a cartoon strip is taped to the inside of his cap.
- **Those who insist on carefully removing and folding every item of excess clothing and placing it lovingly onto the overhead shelf.** It takes forever before they sit down, usually to read their broadsheet papers.

- **The commuters who have their breakfast on the train every morning.** They arrange toast, thermos flask and little mug (often china) and only when it is all carefully aligned do they start their meal.
- **Men who guard their bags on their laps even when there is plenty of room above their heads.** When asked if they would like to place bags on the shelf above they refuse. One guy insisted his luggage was left where he could see it. A colleague attempted to move it so he could reach up to place his bag on the overhead shelf to be told "Leave that alone! You can't move my bags. I must see them!" He continued to display his anger at my colleague who suggested he sought stress counselling.
- **Travellers who always work or read for exactly half the journey and sleep the rest**.

These and many others are repeated every day without variation.

Then, as one of my fellow commuters has pointed out to me, there are the wide range of fidgeters who twitch, tap the table, move their legs up and down continuously and whistle tunelessly. The issue is that once you have been sensitised to their behaviour you can't help but notice it time and time again. The behaviours of the Ritualist often take place just within your peripheral vision, which makes them impossible to ignore.

ANNOYANCE RATING

9 – the Ritualist scores highly because of their routine behaviour. If only they could behave differently once in a while you might be able to ignore them. Regrettably you can't. Any behaviour that involves tapping is doubly annoying because of the addition of sound which compounds the distraction. After you have been travelling on the same train for a number of years you can get frustrated with even the most innocuous of behaviours.

RARITY

6 – this Pain is fairly common. Given that many of us commute to the same job or location year after year you can soon spot the habits and rituals of your fellow commuters. I believe it takes about twelve months of continuous commuting before you begin to develop your own ritualistic behaviours. Sports scientists believe it to be fourteen weeks. I lie awake worrying about my ritual. Maybe it's observing and writing about commuters?

SEASONAL VARIATIONS

There are **no seasonal variations** associated with the Ritualist, people are **weird all year round**.

AVOIDANCE / REVENGE STRATEGIES

1. Accept that we are all creatures of habit and develop your own ritual. Try to make it as disturbing as possible.

2. Shake them vigorously and tell them to give it all up and live on a beach.

3. Sit opposite the Ritualist and mirror everything they do. Once you have struck up a rhythm vary its pace and watch as the Ritualist copies your actions.

4. Bring some balloons onto the train, blow them up and burst them to break the monotony.

5. Brush up on Freud and offer a counselling service to disturbed commuters.

☐ Tick here when you have spotted the Ritualist

RATE THE **RITUALIST'S** ANNOYANCE

The Sardine Packer

GENERAL CHARACTERISTICS

Commuting doesn't get as bad as this. The train you are hoping to get pulls into the station, you take a deep breath and look at the carriages as they stream past you. They are not only all full, but full to overflowing. Faces drop along the platform as the recognition dawns that they won't be getting on this train. There is almost a collective sigh. As the doors slide open those on the tightly-packed train gasp for air and many literally fall out – the same way the builder's crack falls out of his ill-fitting jeans as he bends over. The sane people on the platform recognise the futility of even attempting to get on and resign themselves to take the next train or seek alternative arrangements. Apart from... the Sardine Packer. You will hear them before you see them. "Move along please! Can you move right down inside! Excuse me, will you let me on the bloody train?!" They push and shove, elbow, use their case and anything they can to prise themselves onto the carriage. You are already squashed so tight that you can't even get a fag paper between you and the next person, but still they try. The Sardine Packer has a point, after all they have bought a ticket and are entitled to travel. But all sense of realism disappears as they do their utmost to squash themselves into what little space is left. I am sure the Sardine Packer would be more at home on the Tokyo subway, where their role would be legitimised and indeed even welcome. Unfortunately there are many side effects that come with the Sardine Packer. As you get more and more squashed, you get even closer to

the people next to you. And we all like our personal space now don't we? So this is a terrible experience. You avoid eye contact with the people around you. You look down, but all you see are peoples' groins (which may be misconstrued). You look straight ahead and you might have your face in someone's breasts (more fun in the summer than winter, and then probably only if you are male). The only alternative is to look up. In fact if you look around you, you will notice that this is where everyone else is looking. For the Perverts in the carriage, this is a great opportunity to rub up against someone of the opposite sex (see the Pervert), while for those with halitosis it is the break they need to wipe out an entire population with their potent breath (see the Death Breath). One unfortunate traveller told me he was squashed up against a woman who reeked of urine for his entire thirty-minute commute. I really can't see the point of doing this every day. But people who want the right post code will sacrifice anything to social climbing.

ANNOYANCE RATING

1-10 – annoyance will escalate and will depend on where you start your journey. The closer you get to your destination the more likely it is that you will see the Sardine Packer. And, unless you are sitting down, this is one of the most infuriating people you will regularly see on your daily commute. Mind you, for even those of you who have a seat, there will be people treading on your toes, knocking into your knees and almost sitting on your lap as every available space is taken up by your fellow commuters. Cattle are treated better than this, you know.

RARITY

8 – The Sardine Packer is very common and comes out on any station that is between 20 and 25 minutes from its final destination. This is known as the Sardine Packer Zone.

SEASONAL VARIATIONS

The Sardine Packer is seen on **most days apart from the short school holidays**. The summer holidays tend to be too long to see much of a reduction in the numbers of Sardine Packers. During the winter they tend

to be extra large with all the additional layers of clothing, whilst in the summer they will be nice and sweaty, adding to the bodily smells you have to contend with (see the Stinker).

AVOIDANCE / REVENGE STRATEGIES

1. Sit next to a window and ideally at a table.

2. Lean backwards out of the carriage when the door opens to exacerbate the look of over-crowdedness, which should hopefully force the Sardine Packer to move to the next available door.

3. Move outside of the Sardine Packer Zone – who needs an upmarket post code anyway?

4. Take a clove of garlic with you and chew on it furiously as you enter the Sardine Packer Zone.

5. Wrap razor wire around your briefcase and coat so that nobody will go near you for fear of being severely lacerated.

☐ Tick here when you have spotted the Sardine Packer

RATE THE
SARDINE PACKER'S
ANNOYANCE

The Sleeper

I t is surprising how many people sleep on the train and I am no different. I favour the mornings because my place of work is at the end of the line. This means that when the train stops it is time for me to wake up and sprint enthusiastically off to the office. Sleeping on the way home if you don't live at the end of the line is fatal and should be avoided at all times unless you fancy paying a hefty cab fare home. The Sleeper is someone who is tired of life, especially working life. They look drawn and worn out from long hours, early starts and late finishes (compare this with the New Worker). Commuting, I'm afraid, takes its toll. The Sleeper may appear innocuous but they are far from harmless. They will:

* **Snore**
* **Dribble**
* **Block your exit.**

But they can also be a source of amusement for those who fancy a bit of sport. One commuter told me about the time he was travelling home on the last train out of London. He and his friend were sitting in the carriage when a guy got on and said, "I'm going to sleep. Can you wake me up at Southampton?" "Of course, we'd be delighted," they replied. Then when the train reached Winchester, the two tricksters shouted "Wake up, quick, this is your stop!" The poor victim shot bolt

upright and, still in a daze, dashed onto the platform. As the doors shut behind him they could see the look of horror on his face as he recognised that it was not yet his station. Another ruse is to take an instant photo of the Sleeper and tuck into their breast pocket.

When you are sitting next to a Sleeper you have to cope with the noise and especially the involuntary movements as they slumber. As the train jolts from side to side they slide gradually towards you and you may find their open mouth resting on your shoulder. As the dribble starts to seep from the side of their mouth and onto your lapel you have to decide what to do next. You could move, but it is likely they will end up in your lap which could look unseemly and result in your being misconstrued for a pair of Lovers. You could decide to push them aside hoping that they would not fall into the aisle. Or you could place a tissue on your shoulder to mop up the dribble. It's a difficult choice because whatever action you take is embarrassing. When the dribble is combined with foul breath things get even worse (see the Death Breath). The Sleeper presents a particular problem when they are in an outside seat. My heart sinks when a Sleeper sits next to me, as I know I will have to deal with it sooner or later. Invariably they never get off before your stop and as you get closer and closer to your destination your options run through your mind. "If I nudge him in the next five minutes, he'll get the message that I need to get off at the next stop. Maybe I should excuse myself and stand in the aisle for the rest of the journey. At least I'll be able to get off..." Decisions, decisions. This musing is often accompanied by increased levels of anxiety and a raised heartbeat. Then, of course, there is the occasional death, or what I term the Permanent Sleeper. I have heard of people dying on the train and everyone assuming, quite wrongly, that that they were still asleep. I guess in some way they were.

ANNOYANCE RATING
2 – I don't find the Sleeper too annoying because apart from being trapped in by them, I always manage to escape.

RARITY
7 – The Sleeper is pretty common and you tend to see more in the morning than the evenings apart from Fridays when the combination of a long working week and a couple of gin and tonics have a soporific effect.

SEASONAL VARIATIONS
The **party season** often results in a larger number of Sleepers than usual. I think this is down to the combination of alcohol and plenty of dancing.

AVOIDANCE / REVENGE STRATEGIES
1. Sit on the outside seat. If the person next to you sleeps it won't matter.

2. Eat a family-sized packet of crisps rustling the wrapper as much as you can to maximise the noise. This will keep them awake.

3. Place a laptop on the shelf above their head and hope the train dislodges it (this has happened and proved to be highly effective).

4. Carry a cup to catch the dribble then pour it over their head.

5. Pretend you have Tourettes Syndrome and shout expletives every five minutes.

☐ Tick here when you have spotted the Sleeper

RATE THE
SLEEPER'S
ANNOYANCE

The Social Climber

The Social Climber is one of the great bores of today. You meet them in every walk of life and in most situations so, on that basis, you should expect to see them on the train. The Social Climber normally travels with a companion, either another Social Climber or a passive individual with no opinions of their own – a great opportunity for the Social Climber to outshine their comrade. The Social Climber will bore the pants off their companion (and of course off everyone else) with tales of their exploits, their major achievements at work, and where they have been on holiday, which of course is usually luxurious and exclusive. Pity their poor companion who would rather be having their anal sphincter torn out with a boat hook than hearing the same old boring tripe from their friend. I have a Social Climber on my train most mornings. This fellow travels with a passive type who prefers to read his book than listen to the outlandish stories from his somewhat dishevelled escort. "You know the ticket barriers used in the Tube, I programmed them, and I am going to work on those new ones in Japan..." "I am going to emigrate to Australia in the New Year..." He's still there, I'm afraid, and it doesn't look as though he is going anywhere. "Yeah, I'm reading this great management book at the moment, you should give it a try." I haven't seen it again and I don't think he got past the first page. "Of course, it's much better contracting than working as a full-time employee." This Social Climber, as with all others, has a voice that grates and an intellect that matches. He reads the *Daily Mail*,

which explains a lot. What the Social Climber really wants is another Social Climber to duel with, not some passive twonk who looks painfully bored. When you get two together, it gets more and more stupid as they try to outdo each other. "I went on an all inclusive holiday to the Bahamas." "Really, I went to Tobago, to one of those Six Star resorts." I'm thinking of buying my third holiday home in Florida." "Great, I've just bought my fifth." "OK, I have booked myself onto one of those space flights with the Russian Cosmonauts." "Hmm, I am going to be brought back to life using cryogenics after I'm dead." And so it goes on. Each tries to outdo the other with more and more ridiculous statements about what they have done or what they intend to do. It always seems that the Social Climber has done everything better than everyone else. The reality of course, is that both drive heaps, live on poor housing estates and live their grim lives in a fantasy world. That's the world of the Social Climber. If they were already up there, there would be no point in discussing it. And if they were really that good, just ask yourself why they are travelling standard class and why they don't dress properly. The Social Climber likes to know that other passengers can hear their conversation because it boosts their otherwise tiny ego. Then there are the Social Climbers who have to resort to mobile phones because they have no friends. They like to shout their latest wonderful news down the phone. As with all other Social Climbers, the topics are extreme. For example, one conversation that was overheard recently involved a fifty year old bore (a real old fart) informing the person on the other end of the phone that he was due to see Prince Charles at St. James Palace and that he *had* to go in order to shake his hand. He then went on to discuss how desperate he was for a shag. The reality was that all he would get that evening was a hand shandy.

ANNOYANCE RATING

6 – the problem with the Social Climber is that you cannot help but listen in, as the conversation is loud enough to draw your attention. So if you are trying to work or read it is exceptionally difficult to concentrate on what you are doing.

RARITY

7 – The Social Climber is common. The rise of the middle class means that everyone likes to think they are professional and holds down a responsible job. They are all ambitious and want to accumulate wealth and significant friends. Many are destined to do neither.

SEASONAL VARIATIONS

You tend to find the number of Social Climbers increases significantly around the **holiday seasons**, as each tries to describe why their holiday is bigger and better than everyone else's. Although everyone tries to look impressed, you can see the jealousy in their eyes as they realise their two weeks in Bognor doesn't quite match a safari in Kenya. Not to be outdone, they make up some fantastical trip of a lifetime, which they

patently could not afford without putting themselves into debt.

AVOIDANCE / REVENGE STRATEGIES

1. Pack a pair of earplugs and make a huge fuss as you push them into your lugholes when the Social Climber pipes up.

2. Open this book at this page and hold it strategically so that the Social Climber can see it.

3. Memorise the contents of the Guinness Book of Records and start spouting off the records as your own.

4. Interrupt their conversation and mention that you are doing a survey on people who lie about their achievements.

5. Play every conceivable ring tone on you mobile phone.

☐ Tick here when you have spotted the Social Climber

RATE THE
SOCIAL CLIMBER'S
ANNOYANCE

The Spinster

The Spinster is the opposite of the Family. Whereas the Family is disruptive, noisy and a major pain the in backside, the Spinster is detached, unfriendly, unapproachable and distant. Mind you, surely that is the perfect travelling companion for any commuter; after all they say nothing and do nothing. How ideal could that be? But there are drawbacks. First, they look as though they have eaten a lemon and their anal sphincter is about to erupt. Second, they have no real understanding of what's going on around them. And finally they look too aloof for their own good. They sit there, straight-backed, hands on their lap, staring blankly around them and out of the window. The Spinster's outlook on life is very different from normal folk. They have never married, never had children (or indeed sex) and have probably spent most of their life as a librarian, an accountant or internal auditor. In other words they exude lifelessness. One Saturday during August we decided to venture into London. It was a glorious day and as usual the kids were excited. We sat on the only available seats, three of us at a table and my wife on her lonesome. I sat with the two children. Opposite my daughter was a prime example of the Spinster. She sat there in her tweed jacket and skirt with what looked like a hessian blouse. Prim and proper, pursed lips and sour-faced. My son and daughter, like most youngsters, have a problem with remaining still for more than two minutes. After a short while both were fidgeting and messing around. Nothing too boisterous, you understand, but just

enough for the odd intervention from yours truly. I could see that the dear old Spinster was getting a tad frustrated with their antics. The kids, of course, thought it was highly amusing. My daughter kept on kicking her, not on purpose, but as a by-product of her activities. The Spinster said nothing until it was time to get off. As she stood up to leave she pointedly said "Mind, little girl!" to my daughter as she barged passed. She almost tripped up, much to our amusement. I can see why the poor lady was upset as we, the Family, are the antithesis of the Spinster. In fact, that got me thinking about the whole Pain phenomenon; we are all pains to each other. Although I might find someone else a pain, I am sure they find me a pain too. That's the beauty. We all like to dismiss our own foibles whilst homing in on those of other people. And they are doing precisely the same. So as you Pain Spot, beware of the other Pain spotters spotting you. One story I heard involved a Spinster and an Engager. The Engager, who was a mildly drunk fifty year old, fancied his chances of pulling a sixty-year-old, dried up prune. He adopted the usual Engager ploy of quizzing the Spinster on every aspect of her life. The Spinster was clearly uninterested and after a few minutes told the man to shut up. This unfortunately failed to deter the Engager who continued his questioning. Eventually the Spinster stood up, smashed the Engager on his temple with her industrial-sized handbag and told him to "f**k off!" So maybe some Spinsters have a bit more spunk than others.

ANNOYANCE VALUE
6 – I guess the Spinster is annoying because they just are. It's difficult to explain really but I suppose it's because they do not appreciate a normal life with children.

RARITY
4 – you won't see many Spinsters on the morning commute, but you might just spot the odd one or two in the evenings and at weekends. I am sure with the number of women who are foregoing childbirth in the favour of a free life, we ought to see a lot more of the tired old Spinster in the future, sitting in rows of tweed jackets and puckered faces.

SEASONAL VARIATIONS
There tend to be more Spinsters in the **summer** when they feel able to leave their cocooned environments.

AVOIDANCE / REVENGE STRATEGIES
1. Adopt the strategy of the Territorialist to ensure no one, not even the Spinster, can sit next to you.

2. Keep your tweed detector with you. Should it go off you know you are in danger of meeting the Spinster.

3. Ask them if they need the toilet.

4. Offer them a copy of the *Joy of Sex* just in case they might fancy a bit, although I'm sure it has been decades since they have.

5. Blow up a condom and pop it over your head – this never ceases to impress.

☐ Tick here when you have spotted the Spinster

RATE THE
SPINSTER'S
ANNOYANCE

The Starer

GENERAL CHARACTERISTICS

There is nowt so queer as folk. The Starer is not necessarily the oddest you might see on a train (see the Nutter), but they are certainly the most disconcerting. Knowing that you have a long train journey ahead of you might suggest it would be a good idea to take something to do: read a book, fill in a crossword, sharpen your kitchen knives, slash your wrists, even sleep. But there are a few who take nothing and do nothing. That is, apart from stare. The Starer will retain the same pose throughout the entire journey. They never smile, their deadpan expression never changes. Why do they do this? I can think of a variety of reasons, including:

* The amoeba encased within their skull has yet to kick in, and they haven't quite figured out if they are dead or alive
* They are perverts who take great pleasure from making people feel uncomfortable
* They find you attractive
* They want to kill you
* They are studying human behaviour as part of their PhD
* The are just downright nosy.

We can discount the majority of these, although in this day and age and considering the poor mental state of many people, they might well want to kill

you. Thankfully we don't live in America. But in most cases the Starer is probably no more than a Pervert. I recall travelling to a client one morning; not on my usual train. There was an otherwise presentable man further along the carriage who sat and stared at me and my colleague. After a few minutes the "why is this idiot staring at us?" question dawned on me. Did he fancy us? Was he fascinated in our conversation? Was he just a moron, whose only function in life was to stare at people? I suggested to my companion that we both stared back and saw what happened. The guy didn't stop staring. It was clear that this was a competition, like the ones you used to have as children where the first one to blink lost. Eventually he got off the train, but clearly was not going to back down (I assumed he was off to see the optician). I recently encountered a man who sat opposite me on the way home. His pose did not change throughout the whole journey. He just sat there, elbow on table, hand on chin staring at the same couple in the carriage. It is always difficult to deal with the starer as you really don't want to catch their eye in the fear that they will punch your lights out or become an Engager. A female colleague on a packed train had a guy who just stared at her. After some time, having grown increasingly uneasy, she pointedly asked him what he was staring at. He replied "did you know that you have hairy arms?" How strange is that? Then there was another woman traveller who encountered the Starer on a lengthy journey. Feeling very uncomfortable after fifteen minutes of having the man's eyes boring into her, she stood up, walked purposefully towards the chap and shouted at him "will you stop staring at me! People like you should be locked up! You bloody pervert!" The man retorted "I'm sorry, I don't know what you're talking about, I'm blind." The women went bright purple, turned around, sheepishly shuffled back to her chair and hid behind her paper never to be heard of again. The moral of the story is, never assume anything (see the Five Golden Rules for Pain Spotting in the Afterword).

ANNOYANCE RATING

7 – this all depends on whether you like being stared at. I guess there are those amongst us who find it quite flattering. I personally find it very disconcerting. Surely the Starer would have the sense to wear dark glasses so that they could stare incognito? But maybe they are just too stupid.

RARITY

2 – The Starer does seem to be quite rare, in so far they don't seem to come out much, or maybe I am not that observant.

SEASONAL VARIATIONS

Summer time will tend to bring out more Starers as the wildlife tends to become more interesting. As the female of the species starts to reduce the amount of clothing she wears the number of Starers increases sharply. I am sure there is a direct correlation. Short skirts, flimsy tops help to bring out the Starer in us all (well, mostly in men). I also believe the Starer hibernates during the winter months.

AVOIDANCE / REVENGE STRATEGIES

1. Always choose a seat that provides no opportunity for anyone else to look at you directly.

2. If you have one, use your broadsheet to hide behind.

3. Produce a couple of cue cards which say "What the f*** are you looking at?!" and "Don't look at me I'm irrelevant".

4. Wear a pair of glasses with fake eyeballs on springs.

5. Bring a red hot poker with you and gouge their eyes out.

☐ Tick here when you have spotted the Starer

RATE THE
STARER'S
ANNOYANCE

The Stinker

GENERAL CHARACTERISTICS

Everyone has their own particular aroma, and some are more pungent than others. It is said that our smell makes us attractive to the opposite sex. That's all well and good, but try and say that when your nose is stuck into the armpit of a Stinker and droplets of sweat are cascading from their shirt sleeves onto your face. The Stinker is another seasonal Pain. Unlike the Hero, the Stinker comes out during those balmy summer months, and especially in the evening after a long hot day at the office. I can't say that I have noticed many smelly people on the morning commute, even when it is hot. I guess I get too early a train and none of my fellow commuters have managed to exert themselves enough to produce bucket loads of sweat. The only possible exception would be the Mammoth, who by dint of their size would have over-exerted themselves on the walk along the platform. When we come to the evening, however, it is a very different story. I think it is important to point out that the Stinker appears to be almost predominantly male. I have yet to meet a female Stinker, but then we're told that women never sweat, they glow. A long time ago a colleague had a particular body odour problem which I believe was medical in nature, with no known cure. This man had the ability to fill a room with his personal tang to the point where you could literally see droplets of sweat suspended in the air. Discussing anything with him involved filling my lungs with fresh air and speaking using only the minimum of my lung capacity. Conversations had to be short and to

the point. I guess he thought I was businesslike. What he didn't know was that I didn't want to die. Train travel with him was always something to be avoided, as you felt obliged to sit next to the poor chap. The looks we used to get. I wished I had an sign on my head reading "It's him, not me". On the other hand, it was a great way to get both space and some peace and quiet, as people wouldn't last very long before they turned green and moved on *and* he never said a word throughout the journey. Space and peace, how wonderful. I was tempted to suggest he visit a blacksmith to get his armpits cauterised. Never did though. Other commuters have mentioned stories of people who smelt of rotting flesh, urine, vomit, babies (which for the Spinsters or people without children among you is pooh and sick) as well as many other appalling stenches. A friend of mine regularly sits next to a woman who smells of sweat and burnt toast. Being squashed on a train home on a summer's evening is possibly the worst experience you could ever ask for. Let's face it, you have nowhere to turn, as in every direction you have the sweet stench of sweat or the acrid stink of urine. In such a confined space it seems that everyone smells. Then there is the person who slips off their shoes on the way home. The pong of Camembert drifting down the carriage makes you yearn for a glass of claret. Why do people have to do this? Feet are hardly a person's finest attribute at the best of times, and they certainly hit rock bottom after being confined in tight-fitting shoes during a scorcher of a day. Please go home and subject your family to this niff, not the whole of the train.

ANNOYANCE RATING

4 – this is really a matter of personal hygiene. There are people who love the whiff of freshly produced sweat but I think for the majority of us, this is not the case. Also, if you happen to be on a very packed train in the summer then I can imagine that the relatively low score will rapidly rise, especially if you are squashed between multiple Stinkers.

RARITY

5 – the Stinker is a hot climate phenomenon. So on that basis they are neither very common nor very rare, although I wish they were almost non-existent.

SEASONAL VARIATIONS

The Stinker thankfully only comes out in the summer and their intensive odour usually disappears with the onset of Autumn. Unfortunately, the prospect of a warmer climate as global warming takes hold is a daunting prospect for those of us with sensitive olfactory glands.

AVOIDANCE / REVENGE STRATEGIES

1. Sit next to an open window.

2. Put a peg on your nose.

3. Offer the Stinker the use of your deodorant.

4. Spray air freshener in a circular movement around your seat.

5. Wear an army surplus gas mask and shout "gas attack" as the Stinker boards the train.

☐ Tick here when you have spotted the Stinker

RATE THE **STINKER'S** *ANNOYANCE*

The Stretcher

Everyone says that it is a real drag being short. But this has a distinct advantage on the trains as there is barely enough legroom for the vertically challenged, let alone anyone of medium height or taller. Once again the designers of the rolling stock have failed to study the evolution of the Human Race. Just as we all turning into fatsoes, we are also getting taller. I pity the tall fat person (and the person sitting next to them). So we have to accept that tall people do have a problem, but they do have this terrible tendency of becoming a Stretcher. Stretchers are commuters who love pushing their legs out as far as they can. From the top of their head to the tips of their toes the like to see just how much room they can occupy without leaving their seat. Not satisfied with sharing half of the available space with the person opposite them they want it all. They are the below-the-waist equivalent of the Territorialist. The Stretcher's territorial behaviour involves using every tactic possible to get your legs out of the way of theirs. They will kick you, shove you and push your feet to one side. When they fail to win the battle beneath the table they will stretch out into the aisle and into the seats opposite. This of course presents problems to anyone attempting to navigate along the carriage. As people trip over their legs and knock into them they shoot incredulous looks at the perpetrator. People often become involved in a tussle with the Stretcher, kicking their feet, banging their knees and even resorting to stretching their legs out. A colleague of mine admitted to being a Stretcher with

unintended consequences. As he stretched out his legs and flung back his head and arms behind him he managed to clock the woman behind him on her head. Then there is the variant of the Stretcher that likes to stretch their legs onto the seat opposite, although this tends to be associated with youths and women more than men. And women have a tendency to take their shoes off, which is very unpleasant during the summer. I heard of one story about a Stretcher who met a Reservist on the way home one evening. The Stretcher, in true fashion, had placed their feet on the seat opposite but these shoes looked and smelt as though he had walked in some dog s**t. The Reservist appeared and told the guy that the seat on which he had his feet was his. The guy shot him a look and said "Find someone who cares." As we know, the Reservist (a.k.a. the Terminator) will take offence at such a reaction, which he did. "Get your bloody feet off my seat, you toe rag!" he yelled. Still the Stretcher failed to act. The Reservist threw his laptop case onto the seat and with a loud crack it hit the shins of the Stretcher, who leapt from his seat and pushed the Reservist. Very soon this tussle got out of hand and another couple of people intervened, and eventually the guard was called. The guard managed to sort out the problem and everything seemed fine. However, during the fracas the dog mess managed to find its way onto the seat and the Reservist's laptop bag. As the Reservist sat down he realised what had happened and launched another attack onto the luckless Stretcher opposite, this time smearing the excrement onto the guy's jacket. Soon another fight broke out.

ANNOYANCE RATING
8 – with so little room to go round they have the capability to cause significant damage to you lower body. Just because they are tall does not give them the right to have more than their fair share of the available legroom.

RARITY
5 – the Stretcher is neither very rare or very common, but down the middle. You will come across them daily. Scientists believe that we are all getting taller and I guess if we look back two or three hundred years, when most people were midgets, I think they are probably right. Perhaps in a couple of hundred years from now when everyone is ten feet tall we'll all be Stretchers. We can of course expect that the rolling stock will still be designed for children.

SEASONAL VARIATIONS
The comings and goings of the Stretcher has **nothing to do with the seasons**. These people are just too tall for the trains. Either the trains are going to have to get bigger, or tall people will have to become more considerate. Neither stands much chance of happening.

AVOIDANCE / REVENGE STRATEGIES
1. Never sit at tables or where seats are arranged opposite each other.

2. Always sit opposite a dwarf.

3. To avoid injury and to inflict as much damage as you can to the Stretcher wear knee pads, shin pads and steel toe-capped boots

4. Fix a wooden board to you feet so that when you sit down, the Stretcher is not able to invade your space.

5. Use a chainsaw to cut the Stretcher's legs off at the knees.

☐ Tick here when you have spotted the Stretcher

RATE THE
STRETCHER'S
ANNOYANCE

The Territorialist

GENERAL CHARACTERISTICS

The Territorialist is someone who likes space – especially table space. They need to show they are in control and that no one, but no one, can invade their liberty. Not satisfied with maintaining possession of their own space, they also want to invade yours, like a latter-day dictator desperate to increase their empire, or in this case, their twice-daily empire. There are many theories as to why the Territorialist behaves in the way they do. Some anthropologists see it as a throwback to our Neanderthal ancestors, others believe it is the behaviour of the Alpha Male, needing to dominate the weaker members of the herd. Others yet will put it down to personality profiles and wax lyrical about the differences between introverts and extroverts. All are feasible explanations, but I think it is down to the combination of a small genitals and tiny train tables.

As is often the case, the Territorialist is usually a man. But, with an increasing number of high-powered women executives, it won't be long before their testosterone-enhancing lifestyles will lead to similar territorialist behaviours. I have already noticed many more women with facial hair, so the transformation may have already begun. So if you see a woman dressed in a red power suit sporting a rather nice moustache, find another seat. The Territorialist adopts a number of strategies to encroach on your space and protect it from counterattack. These include:

- **The strategic placement of personal items**, especially bags (why they don't use the luggage racks?).
- **Using elbows** (see below and the Elbow Competitor)
- **Spreading out work papers,** sometimes over the entire table
- **Covering the table with their broadsheet paper** (and sometimes tabloids)
- **Pushing their laptop into your half of the table** and placing their papers on the space next to them, thereby taking up most of the available space.

The more extreme will place other objects such as pictures of their family, wire mesh in trays, staplers, paper clips, coffee mugs and Thermos flasks. These and the many other strategies adopted are highly successful mainly because few who have their space stolen by the Territorialist fight back.

One commuter told me of what he calls the Elbow Competitors who are often seen on trains that feature armrests separating the seats. This is the guy who, by determined stealth, wants to win the prize of the armrest. After the new territory is secured he will hold his elbows firmly in place and refuse to budge an inch, no matter how uncomfortable it may be for the passenger next to him. He'll even avoid turning the pages of his newspaper if it means losing his coveted prize and then to top it all will often turn into the Sleeper or a fully fledged Broadsheet. The fun usually starts when you have two High-Fliers opposite each other. Both vie for as much space as possible, and are destined to have the battle of the laptops. When in full swing, you would be hard-pressed to slip a fag paper in the space between them.

ANNOYANCE RATING

6 – The Territorialist falls into middle of the annoyance spectrum and how much they irritate you depends on whether you want to use the table or place your arm on the rest. For those of us who choose to work, or are forced to by our evil employers, the blood pressure can rise significantly. But what really pisses people off the most are the bloody Broadsheets who leave their papers all over the table.

RARITY

7 – The Territorialist can be spotted more and more often. This is due to the increasing prevalence of laptop computers, the need to work on the morning and evening commutes and to catch up on the latest broadsheet news.

SEASONAL VARIATIONS

Spring brings out more Territorialists than any other season. In the winter people are too tired, depressed and weak to become embroiled in territorial disputes. In the autumn we are all longing for the summer departed and disheartened at the prospect of the winter fast approaching, though we may still be up for some token posturing. In the summer, no one wants to get anywhere near other people because so many of them stink.

AVOIDANCE / REVENGE STRATEGIES

1. Never work on a train and always read a novel.

2. Gradually push your laptop/papers across the table and force the Territorialist to take evasive action before their papers fall onto the floor.

3. Offer to remove their rubbish to the bin and when they react state that you thought they were just littering the carriage.

4. Sew a pin into the elbow of your suit jacket and carefully place you arm on the armrest.

5. Carry a very large and exceptionally heavy suitcase and place it on the table in front of you. That way you can become the ultimate Territorialist.

☐ Tick here when you have spotted the Territorialists

RATE THE **TERRITORIALIST'S** ANNOYANCE

The Texter

We are a nation of texters. More than 16 billion text messages are sent every year. A staggering 45 million messages are sent every day. The Texter is the poor person's Mobile Phoner. Sending a text is significantly cheaper than making a phone call. Wonderful. It's every commuter's dream. No more fools shouting down their phone conducting inane conversations with anyone who will listen. To an extent, I agree. However, the Texter is a bona fide Pain and here's why. They sit with the phone either cradled in their laps or in the palms of their hands, furiously tapping away. Each depression of the key makes a clicking sound. Not particularly loud but sufficient to interrupt your reading or thinking. Relief from the clicking is short-lived as it is soon followed by a "beep" which heralds the despatching of the text. A couple of minutes later, they receive their reply; again indicated by another "beep". The Texter may laugh at the content of the response which is also irritating because you are unaware of the joke. Then it's head down as they create their next message, face contorted through a combination of having to think for the first time ever and the dexterity required to key the message in. Between messages their faces are as blank as an empty sheet of paper. Although initially restricted to the young (on the basis that they can't afford to make real phone calls) colleagues are now so into texting that it is fast becoming the only way you can communicate with anyone. Who says

conversation is dead? Clearly it is, as according to recent research, most youths prefer text messaging to talking – thank God, no more youths on the train blabbing down the phone. What is even better is that many conduct their love lives through text messages too. Although yet to cause a problem on trains, texting is known to cause some interesting issues, which the following illustrate:

- An Italian man threw his wife out of a second floor window after rowing about the number of text messages she was sending.
- One in three people have sent messages to the wrong person. For example, one man texted a friend to find out the name of a girl he fancied, only to find that he sent it to his current bit of fluff.
- Most partners regularly go through their other half's inbox to look for illicit and sexy messages.
- Islamic authorities will prosecute Malaysian men who try to divorce their wives by text.

It won't be long before the embattled commuter can seek his revenge by texting the many Pains who disturb his journey. Maybe this is a Pain worth fighting for? Then again, maybe not.

ANNOYANCE RATING
8 – The Texter wouldn't annoy me so much if they could turn down the volume. The constant stream of key clicks and beeps is enough to drive a saint insane. Mercifully research has found that most will end up suffering from repetitive strain injury. So both the Texter and Mobile Phoner are in store for a miserable future. Is this what we are paying our National Insurance for? I wonder what will happen to those who use third generation mobile technology? Maybe they'll go blind.

RARITY
6 – The Texter is increasingly common although mainly restricted to the young. But you will find an increasing number of quite sane people using it to look hip and save money.

SEASONAL VARIATIONS
Just after Christmas is a good time to spot a larger number of Texters as this is when Santa will have delivered another few million handsets.

AVOIDANCE / REVENGE STRATEGIES
1. Look for a mobile free carriage and enforce the rules.

2. Offer the Texter a splint and point out that without it they will develop repetitive strain injury.

3. Grab hold of their phone and smear half a pound of lard over it.

4. Bring a Braille machine and type your own form of text message.

5. Get hold of their phone number and text them "YDUFO" I am sure they'll get the message.

☐ Tick here when you have spotted the Texter

RATE THE **TEXTER'S** ANNOYANCE

The Toff

Have you ever wondered how the upper classes learn to speak? They all sound identical. Their dialect is like no other. Conceivably they may have been taught to speak this way by mater or pater, by an evil elocution instructor or from having a tablespoon stuffed in their mouth from an early age. The end product is always the same; someone who just sounds stupid. But it's not only the way they speak; it's what they say. They use childish words and silly statements like 'smashing' and 'jolly good'. This is the Toff, the stuff of Billy Bunter, public school and the Old School Tie. The Toff wanders through the carriage with an air of superiority like no other. They look at you as if you were a dog turd they have trodden in. Such unjustifiable snobbery knows no bounds. It's certainly more difficult to spot the Toff. In the past, they would wear their pinstriped suit, bowler hat and even top hat. These days they dress much the same as the rest of the population. What gives them away, however, is the sound when they open their mouths. The Toff is the upper class equivalent of the Gaggle. I sat across from a couple of Toffs one evening and watched their behaviour. Like most Toffs they seemed to have a childish air about them, though they were clearly in their forties. Two ladies the other side of the aisle had to tolerate their approaches. "Ladies, have a glass of champagne." "No, thank you," the women replied politely. "In that case we'll have to throw it away," said the Toffs. They got up, proclaimed loudly "we're on a mission" then walked off down the carriage leaving the

remaining Moet & Chandon and scallops on the table. This balding chap and his mate, who looked remarkably like the lead singer of Erasure, had no hope of pulling. They thought they could impress because they spoke in posh accents and had money. They wound their way to the buffet car, leaving the women passengers in peace. Another time I travelled with three guys who were off to a Toff's weekend. Shooting., polo, and getting drunk on champagne were all on the agenda. Not satisfied with mouthing off about their weekend, they spent the rest of the time talking about their salaries. The Toff likes to brag about their lifestyle, mummy and daddy, and about how much they earn. They are also very uptight and anally retentive – a characteristic they share with the Spinster. As the landed gentry die off and their offspring have fewer or no children (partly due to inbreeding) the Toff should eventually disappear.

ANNOYANCE RATING

8 – I'm afraid the Toff is annoying because of their haughty taughty voice.

Perhaps if they spoke properly they wouldn't be so hated.

RARITY

3 – As the population has drifted towards middle class, either because people have dragged themselves up from the gutter or have fallen on hard times, the numbers of Toffs have reduced and, with the social conditioning that is so prevalent in today's society, they should reduce still further. However, you should expect to see countless Toffs if you commute into London, as this is where the majority will congregate. Having travelled the country it is exceptionally rare to hear the dulcet tones of the upper class lilt anywhere else; it doesn't quite work with a Scouse or Geordie accent. You should also see a lot of Toffs when the theatres chuck out (a fundamentally different experience from when the pubs chuck out their clientele). And of course first class will be packed with them.

SEASONAL VARIATIONS

You should expect to see much more of the Toff during key T**off events** such as **Henley**, **Wimbledon** and **Glyndebourne**. And, of course if you happen to commute anywhere near the Toff's seats of learning like **Cambridge** or **Oxford** you might see more than your fair share.

AVOIDANCE / REVENGE STRATEGIES

1. Avoid any train that coincides with a concentration of Toffs, such as around the time theatres close, for example.

2. Always travel standard class.

3. Wear a tie from Eton to see if you get noticed and when asked say that you were expelled.

4. Place a couple of plums in your mouth so that you can speak in the same way.

5. Wear a Class War T-shirt and walk around first class looking menacing.

☐ Tick here when you have spotted the Toff

RATE THE **TOFF'S** ANNOYANCE

The Train Timer

GENERAL CHARACTERISTICS

It's a sad fact that few trains leave on time. It's even sadder that so many people want to talk about it. Train spotting per se is a strange way to spend your spare time. I could never see the benefit of standing at the end of a cold and wet platform writing down the numbers of passing trains and growing animated at seeing a rare one. Just how mind-numbing can you get? But it looks as though they will be banned because of security concerns. Amazingly this will affect over 200,000 people in the UK alone. If there were to be a prize for the most dull Pain it has to go to the Train Timer. The Train Timer is someone who has spent their entire career commuting on trains. They have been at it for so long that they have pretty much memorised the minutiae of the timetable for the line they travel. Not only do they know the departure and arrival times, they like to discuss them with their travelling companions and anyone else for that matter. There is one train I travel on occasionally which has a couple of middle-aged men on it on it who often discuss the progress of the train. "Well, it's running three minutes later today," says one. "Ah, but that's better than yesterday isn't it? It was seven minutes late," comments the other. They decide to bet on whether it will lose any more time or will make it up. Do people really lead such fruitless existences that discussing the times of trains is their only source of pleasure? A friend told me of a group of train spotters on the way home one evening. The four men (yes, it is another male pursuit, this one) looked dishevelled. Each one carried a tatty hard-

backed notebook containing the product of years of observations. They earnestly discussed the trains they had spotted and then moved onto the subject of the train they were currently travelling on. "This one left late didn't it?" one said. "Yes, it did. Not sure of the reason," said another. And so it went on. What is bemusing is that train drivers themselves join in. "I would like to apologise for the late arrival of this train. We are arriving two minutes late." Then when the train is on time or – God forbid – early, "I'm pleased to inform you that the train is arriving early today!" It is such an achievement that it deserves some special attention from the train crew. Equally disappointing are the outbreaks of spontaneous applause and laughter that ripple through the carriage at the prospect of an early arrival. As an example of social conditioning, this is extremely worrying. Another topic that excites the Train Timer is the compensation payments which the train operating companies have to pay when they fail to meet punctuality targets. Such discussions are just as dull.

ANNOYANCE RATING

7 – the Train Timer is annoying because they are so dull. Listening in on conversations about how punctual or not a particular train is, is hardly scintillating.

RARITY

4 – there are quite a few Train Timers around and they can often be found in Cliques where the same group has travelled together for months or years. You also get the odd Engager who uses the tactic of discussing train times as a way of opening the conversation with their unsuspecting victim.

SEASONAL VARIATIONS

For some reason trains tend to become more punctual in warmer weather so on that basis you ought to expect a slight drop in the numbers of Train Timers. So if you want to catch this one, come out during the **winter**. That said, the Train Timer will get very excited if the trains run to time because they can then introduce some off the wall statistical analysis of punctuality.

AVOIDANCE / REVENGE STRATEGIES

1. Avoid people who carry a train timetable.

2. Pose as a canvasser and ask them their views on the usability of train timetables.

3. Engage the Time Timer in a conversation about how our punctuality compares with other countries and then yawn to show how bored you are at their comments.

4. Pull their timetable from their hands, rip it up and shout "Get a life!"

5. Pull the emergency cord so that they can discuss how late the train is.

☐ Tick here when you have spotted the Train Timer

RATE THE
TRAIN TIMER'S
ANNOYANCE

00:00:0

The Traveller

It is said that travel broadens the mind. Well, so long as I don't have to hear the constant swanking about the places people have been or deal with their luggage and other travel paraphernalia. If someone wants their point of view heard, they raise their voice. This is particularly the case with people who travel a lot. Their posing is exceptionally trying for a number of reasons. First and foremost, it interrupts people reading, writing or thinking. There's no need to shout when someone is fewer than twelve inches away, unless they are stone deaf. Secondly, no one wants to hear why you should visit the Taj Mahal or how friendly the Samoans are. If we wanted to know, we would find out first hand and not rely on a trumped up bore like the Traveller. And lastly, it is a pathetic behaviour. The Traveller likes to think that because they have travelled it makes them an interesting conversationalist. To be interesting, you have to be interested in other people. The Traveller is not. They are egocentrics who love to boast and hold court with their less travelled companions. Their sole purpose is to impress and make those who don't or can't travel feel inferior. They also like to think that they have something profound to say about their cultural experiences, when all they spout is complete and utter bollocks. Let's face it, spending two weeks chilling out in India does not make you an expert on the Indian subcontinent. A friend of mine was on their train home one evening when they had to listen to the tales of a group of three people: some old fart, his bint and, by the look of it, an exchange student.

Throughout the journey they learned about "How wonderful India was", that "the next time you are in Barcelona, you really must visit the museums" and how "fantastic it was to see how the Kenyans live". A long list of places this tired and tedious couple had been. Not satisfied with these fatuous statements, they had to include superfluous interjections about "How I would have loved to have seen such and such, but I was attending an important reception with the Mayor of New York," and "Flying first class is a real luxury". Non-stop drivel from a pair of non-stop jet-setters. Then you get the businessman who has just come back into the country after some important trip. They crow about such things as "the combination of long flights… you just don't know how tired you get" and "I can't tell you how wonderful it all was, there is so much to tell you that I will have to do it when I have more time". Never content to keep it to themselves, they love to tell everyone (see also the High-Flier).

Travellers carry more than their fair share of luggage, either huge suitcases or enormous rucksacks. Indeed, the Rucksacker is one especially insidious variant of the Traveller. These people are unaware that they take up twice the floor area, and because they don't have nerves grafted into the rucksack, are oblivious to it bashing the heads of those who are seated. But the worst thing is that they particularly prone to performing pirouettes, when they need six times the area of one person. A friend of mine was once struck on the temple by the wheel of a skateboard poking out of the top of one of these pirouetters. The Rucksacker is typically an unemployable student or aging hippie who has never quite made it into the mainstream. They normally sport scraggy beards, smell, wear filthy, ill fitting clothes and when they finally realise they cannot fit their rucksack onto the overhead storage they balance it on their laps or fill up the aisle.

ANNOYANCE RATING

8 – I'm afraid the Traveller scores high on the annoyance rating because of the way they have to raise their voices to demonstrate how worldly wise and well-travelled they are. (I find it terribly dull to hear of peoples' travels and how enlightened they feel as a result.) So too does the Rucksacker mainly because they pong, look as though they could do with a damn good wash and have no regard for the wretchedness they cause.

RARITY

5 – We ought to be grateful that the Traveller does not appear as often as some of the other Pains. Most days pass by without seeing any Travellers at all, but Fridays normally bring them out. Here you get the people who are visiting their friends for the weekend, or going off to the airport for a weekend of sun, sea and the inevitable sex.

SEASONAL VARIATIONS

The real fun takes place during the **peak holiday season**. Not only do you get the hip hop, smelly students, but you also get the overseas visitors who are unfamiliar with our railway system getting on the wrong train and trying to communicate in a foreign language to someone who can barely speak English let alone their language. Still it is always good to have fun at their expense by telling them they are on the right train when they are the wrong one and then getting off before they do.

AVOIDANCE / REVENGE STRATEGIES

1. Sit on the inside seat to avoid being battered and bruised by the Traveller's luggage.

2. Carry a Lonely Planet guide to the most obscure place on earth to make the Traveller feel inadequate.

3. Leave photographs from your last holiday lying on the table.

4. Slash their rucksack open with a Bowie knife.

5. Casually leave your leg across the aisle and trip them up.

☐ Tick here when you have spotted the Traveller

RATE THE
TRAVELLER'S
ANNOYANCE

The Vomiter

The Vomiter is to evening as the Broadsheet is to morning. Like the Broadsheet, they venture out only at one end of the day and rarely in between. The Vomiter is usually someone who has been out on the pop for most of the evening (often for the majority of the day). They arrive on the last train home fully tanked up, carrying their cans of Special Brew, Tennent's Super or Cider, incoherent and loud as they stagger through the carriage to find their seat. Of course the Vomiter is not restricted to the hard-core drinkers in society as many will have overdone it with Australian Chardonnay, Harvey Wallbangers and shorts. Once they sit down it is only a matter of time before they start to turn grey and their eyes take on that worried look. It's time to look away or run before they start to bring up the contents of their stomach. As it streams out, covering their trousers, the seat and sometimes other commuters, you see their fellow passengers wince and retch as they hold back their own automatic responses. I had the misfortune to be on the Waterloo and City line in London one Christmas. I couldn't understand why the carriage was empty at one end and packed at the other. As I almost slid along a thick puddle of vomit I discovered why. Before I had the chance to get off and onto another carriage, the doors shut. I thought to myself, could I hold my breath for the five minutes it would take for the train to reach its destination? Some hope. The smell alone was enough to make anyone without a strong constitution throw up. The guy, who had probably looked terribly smart when he

walked out of the door at seven in the morning, was certainty a picture now. His Armani suit (he was a City Boy) was replete with a splash (literally) of orange (the diced carrot), and Chartreuse yellow from his bile. Everyone was trying to ignore him; difficult when he is fewer than three feet way. I am sure his suit was ruined. My financial advisor was travelling home one evening, not particularly late, on what he calls the Vomit Comet. One passenger joined the train completely drunk and as he staggered along the compartment clutching his can of beer he chundered. He offered a passable imitation of a muck spreader as his vomit sprayed out, covering himself and everyone around him. He began to smear the remnants around his face and into his hair, oblivious to what had happened. A couple of guys, who for some strange reason happened to have some water pistols rushed to the toilet and filled them up. On their return they began squirting the Vomiter on his head. It had the desired effect. The guy who had been sick spent the rest of his journey rubbing yet more vomit into his hair and around his face, to the great merriment of the rest of the carriage. So, sometimes, Pains can be a source of amusement. As soon as I mentioned this Pain to my colleagues, out came yet more examples, which included one chap's wife spewing into a spare pair of stockings on the Docklands Light Railway, before popping the squashy package neatly back into her briefcase, and another where a backpacker was violently ill into a carrier bag containing new sweaters. The Vomiter is certainly inventive.

ANNOYANCE RATING

10 – The visual effect alone is sufficient to make the Vomiter a top scorer when it comes to annoyance. If people can't take their drink they shouldn't drink at all. Being drunk is one thing, but creating a pavement pizza on a train is clearly overstepping the mark. But the worst aspect of the whole experience is the smell. The stench of freshly-brewed vomit is not the most pleasant of odours and is not the sort of thing you would like to smell after a nice meal or evening out.

RARITY

4 – Thankfully, the Vomiter is quite rare. You have to be a night owl to spot them, or someone who has no choice, because of shift work, but to travel on the last few trains home of an evening. Friday nights tend to be a good time to spot them, as this is when the majority of them come out – to celebrate another miserable and pointless week at work.

SEASONAL VARIATIONS

Any party season tends to bring out more Vomiters than normal, and Christmas is often a great time to see them travel in

groups. I wonder what the correct term is for a group of Vomiters? Perhaps it's a Spray?

AVOIDANCE / REVENGE STRATEGIES

1. Do your utmost to get an early train.

2. Carry a sick bag with you and pass it out to the Vomiter before his throws up. They will love you for it and so will your fellow passengers.

3. Save your poncho the next time you go to a theme park, such as Thorpe Park. When the Vomiter gets on the train, whip it out.

4. Take a digital camera with you, photograph the Vomiter, find out where he works and post his image on the company website.

5. Get drunk so that you won't notice, or remember a thing the next day.

☐ Tick here when you have spotted the Vomiter

RATE THE
VOMITER'S
ANNOYANCE

The Wheeled Caser

GENERAL CHARACTERISTICS

As a boy growing up in a Hertfordshire market town I used to see old ladies walking home from town with their little trolleys stuffed full of fresh bread and other produce carefully selected from the array of shops they visited. These were colourful things which afforded the old dears that used them some additional stability and stopped them from toppling over. We even had one old lady who would carry her shopping in bags so that she could transport her dog around in the trolley. Many years later, and much to my surprise, I noticed the re-emergence of the trolley. Not with the aged amongst us, but among the professional classes. Walking round the major cities of the UK I saw young thrusting executives pulling their work in trolleys behind them. Starting quite small, perhaps the size of a modest briefcase, these soon grew to be much larger. Some now look more like the luggage you would take on holiday than drag to a day at the office. Why they can't carry a case? I suspect they have weak spines. This causes those of us who have modest needs a number of problems, including:

- **Taking up more than their fair share of luggage space.** The trolley is a lot larger than the average case and so will not fit on the overhead shelf. This gives the Wheeled Caser three options. They can block up the aisle, they can use the seat next to them or they can pop it in front of their feet.

- As the Wheeled Caser trundles along the station platform they have this terrible tendency of **running over the feet** of anyone who happens to get in their way. Carnage follows in their wake.
- Moving through the carriage also proves difficult because the trolley is often wider than the aisle. **The Wheeled Caser, undeterred, will force their way through the train.** In their path they leave bruised feet, legs and arms as well as plenty of red faces.

The Wheeled Caser also has the ability to frustrate getting on and off the train too. In both cases they insist on fiddling with the handle, either pulling it out or pushing it in whilst a queue of people banks up behind them heaving and sighing whilst this jerk plays around with their trolley. At least it is preparing them for old age. Then, and to add to the misery of their fellow commuters, they storm off, knocking people out of their way as they charge for the exit.

ANNOYANCE RATING

6 – The Wheeled Caser annoys because of the ridiculous way they struggle with their trolley. Forcing their oversized baggage onto rolling stock that was designed for a small briefcase is shear agony for the rest of the commuting population. But so is the total disregard the Wheeled Caser has for those around them.

RARITY

9 – The Wheeled Caser is, I'm afraid to say, a common sight on our trains.

SEASONAL VARIATIONS

None. But, just keep your eyes open at Christmas time when you might spot some additional Wheeled Casers carting off their Christmas goodies.

AVOIDANCE / REVENGE STRATEGIES

1. Sit as near as possible to the larger luggage spaces so that the Wheeled Caser has to use the racks rather than taking up your space.

2. Take up as much space as possible so that the Wheeled Caser has to find somewhere else to sit.

3. Wear clown shoes and block the aisle.

4. Ask to see the contents of their trolley and then quiz them on why they carry so much junk to work.

5. Get yourself a trolley, fit the wheels with James Bond-style knives and see if you can cut the wheels off a passing Wheeled Caser's trolley.

☐ Tick here when you have spotted the Wheeled Caser

RATE THE
WHEELED CASER'S
ANNOYANCE

The Youth

GENERAL CHARACTERISTICS

Why do people want to hold onto their youth? I can't understand why anyone opts for face lifts, Botox and the other invasive procedures required to retain their unblemished appearance. I find this even stranger whenever I come across the Youth because they and their behaviour would make anyone want their pension book immediately. The Youth is generally between the ages of fourteen and eighteen, with no respect for anything or anybody. They sit there, spotty faced, in clothes that no self-respecting tramp would consider, legs on the seat opposite, plugged into a personal stereo and looking smug. The Youth seeks to camouflage a gangly and unattractive body with ill-fitting clothes, make up and zit cream. But the key thing about the Youth is that they like to kick against society and the mainstream. They are contemptuous of anyone older than their mid-twenties and abhor middle and old age in particular. They will behave in a way calculated to shock. So don't expect them to conform to the behaviour of the normal person, or even the average commuter. They will:

- Shout because they have yet to learn how to speak quietly
- Swear because they have such a limited vocabulary that they know no other words
- Stare because there is nothing between their ears
- Pick on people in the carriage (especially when there is a group of Youths)
- Discuss their mates openly so that everyone in the carriage can hear

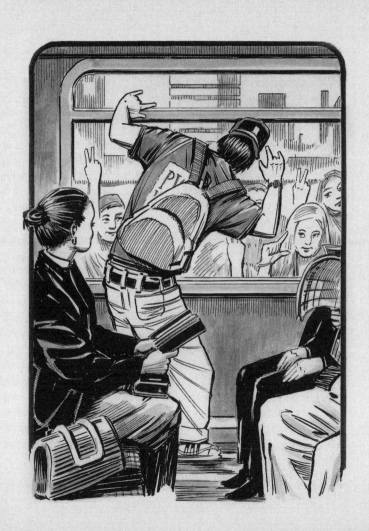

- Boast about their drinking habits
- Discuss sex when they are still virgins
- Commandeer as much of the space around them as possible, usually with their feet.

On one evening's commute, I was sitting across from a Youth. He was tall, very spotty, with his legs on the seat next to me. He was quite well dressed for a Youth and spoke with in a posh accent. Despite his well-to-do nature he still displayed the classic characteristics of the Youth. He was on the phone to one of his mates, discussing as loudly as possible his and all his acquaintances' love lives: "Yeah, Sarah's a right dog. I can't believe she went with James so soon after Simon." After each vignette he would laugh loudly, shuffle his feet on the seat opposite him and move onto to his next subject. "I think that History teacher is a real ponce, I would love to get him the sack… I was so drunk last night I could barely stand; what did I do again?" The conversation was vacuous, pointless and grating. On and on he went, laughing and talking complete tripe, looking around the compartment at the other commuters impervious to their hostile glances. He was loving it, holding court with a load of disapproving old people. After some thirty minutes of this a late middle-aged gentleman stood up, rolled up his evening paper and walked resolutely towards the Youth. As he reached his intended victim he stretched out his arm and smacked the paper smartly round the Youth's head and said "I think we have heard enough of your foul conversation. Turn the bloody phone off and shut up!" With that he turned around and marched back to his seat. The compartment erupted with applause. At long last the Youth had been silenced. The Youth, flushed with shock, whispered hoarsely into the phone "got to go, I'll ring you later". He spent the remainder of the journey looking out of the window nursing a throbbing temple and bruised ego.

ANNOYANCE RATING

7 – The Youth will annoy you for many different reasons. Some commuters wish they still had the balls to behave so badly and not care about it. Others who can't accept that they are nearer the grave than they would like to be detest their adolescence. But for the most of us the annoyance stems from the total disregard for convention and the way they behave. The annoyance can increase significantly when they travel in groups.

RARITY

5 – You won't see much of the youth in the mornings. This is the time when they are still recovering from the wicked time they had the night before. And, of course most still have to go to school. You will see more of them during the late afternoon and evenings, and especially Fridays when they can commence their weekend of underage boozing and fornication. Mind you, as the population ages we should expect to see less of the Youth as they and all their chums grow old and decrepit.

SEASONAL VARIATIONS

You will see much more of the Youth during any **school/college holiday**, especially the summer vacation. There will be herds of Youths taking the train to spend all day roaming the streets of the major conurbations doing nothing but hanging out with their friends, taking drugs, getting drunk and shoplifting. A pointless activity for a worthless cohort in society.

AVOIDANCE / REVENGE STRATEGIES

1. Only ever sit near people who are over the age of forty.

2. Completely ignore them. They won't like this one bit, as they are after attention.

3. Pose as a dermatologist and discuss the severity of their spots.

4. Superglue their mouth up.

5. Dress up as the Child Catcher from *Chitty Chitty Bang Bang* and ensnare them with your net.

☐ Tick here when you have spotted the Youth

RATE THE
YOUTH'S
ANNOYANCE

Afterword

*S*o you have seen them, heard them, smelt them, touched them and no doubt been frustrated by them. Everywhere you look you see Pains. You may have also realised that you too are a Pain and by now have recognised which category (or categories) you fall into. So how do you avoid being a Pain? Here are my top five ways:

1. Pain spot (obviously)
2. Read a novel, any small format book or tabloid newspaper
3. Sleep (but do be careful where)
4. Look out of the window (but make sure you look interested)
5. Meditate

And, finally, here are the Five Golden Rules for Pain Spotting. They will help you live a fulfilled, happy and enriched life.

1. *NEVER JUDGE A BOOK BY ITS COVER*
You mustn't be fooled by initial appearances. What at first glance may seem like a commonplace Engager might actually turn out to be a Phantom Farter, who is talking incessantly to disguise the fact that they are slowing rotting on the inside. Likewise, a straightforward Broadsheet may in fact be a fully-fledged Vomiter. First impressions count, sure, but vomit on your best shoes will leave a much more lasting impression. There's nothing to stop you ticking off more than one 'Pain' per

observation. So, make your observations; do your analysis, and be sure you have got all the qualities of every Pain straight before committing yourself.

2. *DON'T STEREOTYPE*
Pains, like all people in general, can change. So just as a man can become a woman (though surgery), a Broadsheet can evolve into a Nutter (through the long-term impact of commuting). Always watch out for the telltale changes that suggests evolution, like halitosis, uncontrollable farting and a sudden increase in girth.

3. *DON'T BE TOO JUDGMENTAL*
The reasons for this are two-fold. First off, this book is about providing an amusing diversion during train travel. Second, we are all Pains of one form or another, and as the saying goes, 'People in glass houses shouldn't drop their guts on a packed commuter train'.

4. *DON'T GET INTO ANY FIST-FIGHTS*
Any suggestions that 'the book told me to do it' are like a tower of jelly – they won't stand up in a court of law.

5. *LEARN TO LOVE YOUR PAIN*
This is the trickiest and most testing of all the Golden Rules. But you should learn to love the Pain. For he is your brother. Or your 86-year-old incontinent grandmother. The Bible tells us to love thy neighbour. And that means 'unconditionally'. Even when your neighbour's sweaty love-handles are slowly oozing over your armrest. Besides, if you don't learn to love them, you might just go mad.

Pains_on@hotmail.com – Don't forget to send your stories about Pains on the Payroll and Pains in Public.